A TAST

LONDON

by

JENNY LINFORD

PHOTOGRAPHY
BY
CHRIS WINDSOR

A TASTE OF LONDON

Written by Jenny Linford
Photography by Chris Windsor
Edited by Lydia Linford
Design by Metro

Published in 1997 by
Metro Publications
PO Box 6336
London
N1 6PY

Printed in Great Britain by:
The Burlington Press
Foxton
Cambridge

British Library Cataloguing in Publication Data.
A catalogue record for this book is available from the British Library.
ISBN 0952291479

To our son Ben Windsor

ACKNOWLEDGEMENTS

First of all, heartfelt thanks to my nearest and dearest – to my husband Chris Windsor for taking yet more wonderful photographs for a book of mine, to my mother Lydia Linford who both supplied a recipe and proof-read the book and to Sue and Paul Windsor for much loving baby-sitting, looking after our young son Ben, which gave me valuable time to work on this book.

A big thank you also to all the people who so generously contributed recipes to the book: Stella Christofi, Ranu Dally, Gemma Eddington, Raviv Goldman, Lynne Jones, Constant Leung, Lydia Linford, Samar Manzoor, Annabelle Pangborn, Julia Papantonis, Anna Persson, Michael Rimmer, Reena Suleman, Arturo Tosi, Mrs Wong and her daughters Juliana and Vera, and Maria Yiannoullou.

Thank you finally to Andrew and Susi at Metro, without whom this book wouldn't be in print.

CONTENTS

THE AUTHOR

Jenny Linford lived in Ghana, Trinidad, Singapore and Italy before settling in London where she now works as a freelance food writer.

Her previous books include **Food Lovers' London** (Metro), **Writing About Food** (A & C Black) and, as co-author with Michael Driver and Paul King, the **Tate Gallery Cookbook** (Tate Gallery Publications). She is the Teletext Food & Drink Writer and has written articles for **The Guardian, The Time, Taste, Time Out** and **The Evening Standard**.

An Inveterate food-shopper herself, Jenny founded the highly successful **Gastro-Soho Tours** (0181-348 7767) in 1994, guided tours of Soho's diverse food shops from Chinese supermarkets to veteran Italian delis.

INTRODUCTION

Having explored London's multi-cultural foodshops in my guide *Food Lover's London*, the next logical step seemed to be to write a cookbook giving recipes using some of the many exotic or unfamiliar ingredients found in the capital, from fragrant kaffir lime leaves to orange-fleshed kabocha (Japanese pumpkin).

Here, therefore, is a diverse collection of recipes, spanning a number of cuisines from African and Caribbean to Swedish. Some of the recipes are traditional classics, such as Trinidadian callaloo soup, Polish bigos or Thai green curry, while others are cross-cultural creations, such as tindola couscous or wine-baked red snapper. While the majority of recipes are mine, there are also a number of recipes from an assortment of food-loving Londoners, who generously shared their ideas with me.

Shopping for the ingredients to test the recipes in this book brought home to me once again the wonderful wealth and diversity of foodshops which London houses. Stroll through Chinatown in the summer months and one can't help but notice the bundles of wonderfully fresh leafy green Chinese vegetables, bags full of lychees and longans and piles of huge spiky durian outside the supermarkets. Alternately, visit Southall or Ealing Road in Wembley and one finds a staggering range of Asian fruit, vegetables and herbs: from orange, red and green mangoes to bunches of fresh fenugreek or methi.

Sometimes this cornucopia of exotic foodstuffs can be daunting. That's why I've written this cookbook to suggest some simple, delicious ways in which to actually use these unfamiliar ingredients. It's all too easy to stick to what's familiar, but there are a host of delicious ingredients in London simply waiting to be discovered. Don't be daunted – be open-minded and greedy!

A TRIP TO BRIXTON MARKET: NINE RECIPES

LYNNE'S CALLALOO SOUP
CRAB-STUFFED CHRISTOPHENE
OKRA AUBERGINE COCONUT STEW
CHILLI THYME CORN BREAD
SWEET POTATO FISH PIE
GEMMA'S BRIXTON MARKET HOTPOT
PLAINTAIN CHIPS
FRIED PLANTAIN
SORREL JELLY

Brixton Market, unlike many of London's food markets, retains its vitality and exuberant bustle, spilling over from the market arcade itself to the side-streets and railway arches around it. I'm always struck by the colours of the fresh foodstuffs on sale: zingy green limes, orange pumpkins, green, red and orange mangoes. The numerous fish stalls with their displays of red snappers, parrot fish and tilapia are a medley of irridescent blues, pinks, reds and yellows. Customers pick and choose their wares, sucking their teeth in disapproval and tutting loudly at the prices.

African-Caribbean food remains largely unfamiliar to a Western audience, despite shops and markets selling African and Caribbean ingredients all around London from Portobello, Shepherds Bush and Tooting markets to Stroud Green Road in north London. This is a shame as there are a host of delicious fruits and vegetables to be enjoyed, from sweet, starchy plaintain to soursop, a large armour-skinned fruit, with a wonderfully fragrant sherbetty sour-sweetness.

Brixton Market

3

LYNNE'S CALLALOO SOUP

Trinidadian Lynne Jones cooks food from around the world. When cooking for her English friends she cooks Caribbean food but for her West Indian friends she cooks "something different as that's the food they eat at home".

Callaloo soup is eaten throughout the West Indies in different versions. "Some people use salt meat. You can use anything," says Lynne. "This is a Trinidadian version which I've kept quite simple."

Bunches of green callaloo (the leaves of the dasheen or taro plant) can be found in Brixton Market. Spinach is the closest substitute. The soup takes on a piquancy from the green Scotch bonnet pepper which is infused whole with the stock. Lynne uses a green Scotch bonnet "because it's less likely to burst than a ripe red one".

Ingredients (serves six)

450 g/1 lb callaloo leaves
1 onion
1 clove garlic
2-3 spring onions
225 g/8 oz okra
1.3 ltr/2¼ pts chicken stock
¼ tsp chopped thyme
6 tbsp coconut milk
1 green Scotch bonnet pepper
salt and freshly ground black pepper
6 cooked crab claws

Wash the callaloo and chop coarsely. Peel and chop onion and garlic. Trim and chop spring onions (both white and green parts).

Chop the okra, discarding stems. Into a large heavy saucepan put the callaloo leaves, chicken stock, onion, garlic, spring onion and thyme. Bring to the boil and simmer for 10 minutes.

Add in the chopped okra and coconut milk. Bring back to the boil. Add in the green Scotch bonnet pepper and simmer for 20 minutes. Leave soup to stand for a further ten minutes then carefully remove and discard the whole green pepper, being careful not to puncture or burst it.

Blend the soup for one or two minutes, depending on how smooth you would like it. Season with salt and freshly ground pepper. Gently heat soup through. Meanwhile, crack the crab claws removing half the shell. Serve soup piping hot garnished with crab claws.

CRAB-STUFFED CHRISTOPHENE

The christophene (also called cho-cho or chayote or, more poetically by the Chinese, Buddha's Hand Gourd) is a pale green, pear-shaped and sized vegetable. It is a firm-fleshed member of the squash family with an innocuous flavour which lends itself to a savoury filling, just as courgettes and marrows do. Using fresh or thawed, frozen crab meat rather than tinned makes all the difference to the success of the dish.

This makes a tasty first course for four people and is good followed by Wine-Baked Red Snapper (see p.131). Served with rice it makes a meal for two.

Ingredients (serves four as a starter or two as a main course)

2 large christophene
salt and freshly ground pepper
1 onion
55 g/2 oz butter
115 g/4 oz white and brown crab meat
25 g/1 oz grated Parmesan cheese
2 tbsp fresh breadcrumbs

Boil christophenes whole in salted water for around 30 minutes until tender. Drain, slice in half lengthwise, removing the shallow central stone.

Carefully cut out the central christophene flesh, leaving the skin intact. Finely dice christophene flesh. Peel and finely chop onion.

Melt 1 oz/25 g butter in frying pan. Gently fry onion until softened. Mix together christophene flesh, fried onion, flaked crab meat, Parmesan and breadcrumbs. Season with salt and freshly ground pepper. Divide mixture among the four christophene shells, pressing it down into the shells. Dot with remaining butter and bake for ½ hour at Gas Mark 5/375F/190C.

OKRA AUBERGINE COCONUT STEW

The slender green tapered ridged pods called okra (also bhindi or, descriptively, lady's finger) are easy to spot. Choose the smallest freshest looking ones, avoiding those which are discoloured or look tired and old. They have a distinctive glutinous texture which is prized by some and disliked by others. This recipe combines them with the pearly, white-yellow egg-sized globe aubergines sold in African-Caribbean and Asian shops, but ordinary purple aubergine can be substituted.

Ingredients (serves four)

1 clove of garlic
1 cm/½ in root ginger
1 onion
225 g/8 oz okra
1 tbsp oil
6 small white globe aubergines
1 tsp ground cumin
½ tsp ground turmeric
1 tsp ground coriander
1 x 400 ml tin coconut milk
salt
a few sprigs of fresh coriander

Okra

Peel and finely chop garlic, root ginger and onion. Wash and dry the okra to lessen stickiness. Cut the stem cap off each okra pod, being careful not to cut into the pod itself and release its sticky juices. Halve the globe aubergines.

Heat the oil in a casserole dish. Gently fry garlic, ginger and onion until softened. Mix in ground cumin, turmeric and coriander. Add in okra and aubergines and mix well. Pour in coconut milk. Add salt. Stirring, bring to the boil. Reduce heat, partly cover and simmer gently for 30 minutes. Roughly tear coriander sprigs and add to the stew just before serving.

CHILLI THYME CORN BREAD

Cornmeal is one of the many flours sold in African-Caribbean foodshops and makes a delicious, slightly nutty bread. This recipe, adapted from Deborah Madison's seminal vegetarian cookbook *The Greens Cookbook*, is flavoured with aromatic thyme and a slight chilli kick.

Ingredients (makes 1 loaf)

1 small red chilli
2 sprigs of thyme
55 g/2 oz butter
225 g/8 oz cornmeal
225 g/8 oz plain flour
2 tsp baking powder
2 tbsp sugar
1 tsp salt
2 large eggs
300 ml/½ pt milk

Scotch bonnet peppers

AFRICAN & CARIBBEAN

Finely chop chilli, discarding stem. Finely chop thyme. Melt butter. Preheat oven to Gas Mark 6/400F/200C.

Mix together cornmeal, flour, baking powder, sugar and salt in a large mixing bowl. Mix in chilli and thyme.

Beat eggs. Mix with milk and melted butter. Pour the egg mixture into the dry ingredients and mix gently. Be careful not to overmix.

Turn cornmeal mixture into a well-greased 3 x 2 x 8 inch loaf tin and bake for 40 minutes. Serve warm from the oven.

SWEET POTATO FISH PIE

Pink-skinned sweet potatoes have, as their name suggests, a pleasant sweet flavour. Either the white or orange-fleshed variety can be used in this recipe. Use undyed smoked haddock fillet rather than the lurid yellow dyed smoked haddock for the best results.

Ingredients (serves four)

1 kilo/2 lb 4 oz sweet potatoes
salt and freshly ground pepper
1 tbsp lemon juice
300 ml/½ pt milk
55 g/2 oz butter
pinch of freshly ground nutmeg
450 g/1 lb smoked haddock
2 onions
2 celery stalks
1 tbsp olive oil
1 tbsp dry sherry/white wine
½ tbsp flour

Sweet Potatoes

Peel and chop sweet potato. Cook in salted boiling water with 1 tbsp of lemon juice added to it until tender. Drain and mash with a 2-3 tbsp of the milk, 25 g/1 oz butter, salt, freshly ground pepper and freshly ground nutmeg.

Poach the smoked haddock in simmering water for 5 minutes. Remove with a slotted spoon and flake, discarding skin and any bones.

Peel onions and chop into rings. Finely chop celery. Gently fry onion and celery in olive oil until softened. Pour in sherry and cook for a further 2-3 minutes.

Make a white sauce by melting 25 g/1 oz of butter in a thick-bottomed saucepan, mixing in ½ tbsp flour and cooking gently for 2-3 minutes. Gradually mix in the milk and, stirring, bring to the boil until thickened. Season with salt and freshly ground pepper.

Place smoked haddock in ovenproof serving dish. Top with onion mixture. Pour over white sauce. Top with mashed sweet potato. Bake for 45 minutes at Gas Mark 5/375F/190C.

GEMMA'S BRIXTON MARKET HOTPOT

Gemma Eddington, an adventurous and open-minded cook who experiments with dishes from around the world, is a devotee of Brixton Market, "the best in South London". This dish combines ingredients readily found in the market to make a hearty stew. A distinctive kick is given by the presence of Scotch bonnet peppers. These look like small dainty capsicums, ranging in colour from yellow and green to orange and red, and are lethally hot. Handle with care, being sure to wash your hands after touching them. Gemma suggests serving her hotpot with rice and beer, followed by a mango or, for the greedy, bananas fried in butter with a touch of rum.

Ingredients (serves four)

450 g/1 lb chicken pieces
1 little flour
salt and freshly ground pepper
225 g/8 oz okra
2 onions
2 potatoes
½ red pepper
1 clove of garlic
a few sprigs of fresh thyme
1 Scotch bonnet pepper
50 g sachet of creamed coconut
200 ml/7 fl oz chicken stock/hot water
1 tbsp palm oil
1 tbsp tomato puree
1 x 400 g tin chopped tomatoes
1 bay leaf
1 heaped tsp raw cane dark brown sugar

Cut the chicken into bite-sized pieces (If using chicken on the bone, Gemma suggests cutting the meat off the bone and using the bones to make the stock required for the recipe). Sprinkle the chicken pieces with flour seasoned with salt and plenty of pepper.

Wash okra and pat dry. Cut conical caps off the okra, being careful not to cut into the pod itself and release its sticky juices. Peel and roughly chop the onions. Cut the potatoes into 2.5 cm/1 in sq chunks. De-seed and roughly chop the red pepper. Peel and crush garlic. Finely chop thyme, discarding tough stalks. De-seed and finely chop the Scotch bonnet pepper. Dissolve the creamed coconut in hot chicken stock or water.

AFRICAN & CARIBBEAN

9

Parboil the potato chunks and drain. Meanwhile, heat the palm oil in a large casserole dish. Fry the chicken pieces over medium heat. Once they begin to turn brown add in the onion and cook until softened. Reduce heat slightly and add in potato chunks, red pepper, garlic, thyme and Scotch bonnet pepper, mixing well.

Add in the okra and cook for a few minutes, stirring gently now and then. When okra have turned a really bright green mix in the tomato puree, coconut liquid and chopped tomatoes.

Gradually bring to the boil. Add in the bay leaf and sugar. Cover and simmer for 30-40 minutes until chicken is tender and the okra just beginning to split. Season with salt and freshly ground pepper.

PLAINTAIN CHIPS

Sweet-flavoured, starchy plaintain look like huge, ridged bananas but are eaten both as a vegetable and as a fruit. They are sold both unripe, when they are a light green colour, and ripe, when they turn deep yellow with black blotches.
Serve these slightly sweet 'crisps' as a party nibble.

Ingredients (serves four)

2 green plaintains
oil for deep-frying
salt

Top and tail the green plaintains. Cut 4 strips lengthwise down each plaintain, cutting through the skin but not into the actual flesh. Peel off the skin. Slice into fine rounds.

Deep-fry in batches until the plaintain deepens in colour to a golden-brown. Remove with a slotted spoon, drain on kitchen paper, sprinkle with salt and serve.

FRIED PLANTAIN

A simple, pleasant vegetable side-dish.

Ingredients (serves four)

3 ripe plaintains
oil for shallow-frying

Peel plaintains and cut into fine strips about 7 cm/3 in long. Heat oil in a large frying pan. Fry the plaintain strips until golden-brown and serve at once.

SORREL JELLY

Caribbean sorrel or roselle is a bright red fruit, not to be confused with the green leaf of the same name so beloved by the French. Dark red sorrel sepals, sold fresh or dried, have a distinctive tart fragrance and are traditionally used to make a classic Caribbean Christmas drink. In this recipe sorrel is used to make a rich-flavoured, deep red jelly.

Ingredients (serves four to six)

15 g/½ oz leaf gelatine
1 cm/½ in piece of root ginger
55 g/2 oz dried sorrel petals
4 cloves
1 cinnamon stick
600 ml/1 pt cold water
55 g/2 oz caster sugar

Set gelatine to soak in 3 tbsp of the cold water. Peel and grate ginger. Place sorrel, ginger, cloves, cinnamon stick and remaining water in a saucepan.

Bring to the boil. Over a medium heat mix in the caster sugar, stirring until dissolved. Strain sorrel mixture into another saucepan. Mix gelatine into hot sorrel liquid at once, stirring until gelatine is dissolved.

Strain liquid into a serving dish or wetted jelly mould and set aside to cool. Once cool cover and transfer to fridge. Chill until set, around 5 hours.

Plantain

RECOMMENDED BOOKS

Caribbean and African Cookery,
Rosamund Grant.
An evocatively written, informative and accessible cookbook from the owner of the former Bambaya Restaurant in Crouch End.

Caribbean Cooking,
Elizabeth Lambert Ortiz.
An excellent, knowledgeable wide-ranging look at Caribbean cuisine.

Creole Caribbean Cookery,
Kenneth Cardiner.
A well-written cookbook with several appetising recipes.

Nigerian Cookbook,
H.O. Anthonio and M. Isoun.
A very clear, informative book on Nigerian cuisine.

A Taste of Africa,
Dorinda Hafner.
A fascinating look at African and Caribbean cookery, written with exuberance and infectious enthusiasm and crammed with photos and appealing recipes.

Traditional Jamaican Cookery,
Norma Benghiat.
An informative look at Jamaican cuisine, containing recipes for classic dishes such as jerked pork and escoveitch fish.

AFRICAN & CARIBBEAN GLOSSARY

Bitter leaf: an African leaf, related to the lettuce family, with a distinctive flavour available dried or frozen.

Breadfruit: a football-sized fruit with thick, green, pimply skin and creamy flesh, used both as a starchy vegetable and in pies and puddings.

Callaloo: green leaves of the dasheen plant, used to make a famous eponymous soup, available tinned and fresh.

Cassava: large, brown, hand-shaped tubers of the cassava plant, also called manioc or yucca. Bitter cassava, despite containing toxic prussic acid which must be removed by either cooking or pressing, is a staple food. Yellow-fleshed sweet cassava is eaten as a vegetable. Dried, ground cassava is used in Africa to make gari. Ground cassava meal is used in the West Indies to make a type of bread and the flavoured juice of grated cassava is used to make cassareep, a key ingredient of pepperpot.

Catfish, dried: small blackened fish, with a distinctive large head, used to add flavour in soups and stews in West African cooking.

Cho-cho (christophene, chayote): a pear-sized member of the squash family, with a wrinkled skin ranging in colour from white to green and watery white flesh.

Coconut: coconut flesh and milk are widely used in Caribbean cookery.

Cornmeal: coarsely or finely ground dried corn kernels.

Crayfish, dried: although called 'crayfish' in Africa, these are a type of shrimp, used whole or ground as flavouring.

Custard apple: apple-sized fruit with a knobbly, armoured green skin. The white, sweet pulp around glossy seeds has a custard-like texture, hence the name.

Dasheen: potato-sized fibrous tubers, with white starchy flesh. Some varieties of dasheen have an acrid taste.

Eddoe: a small, rounded fibrous tuber, with white starchy flesh.

Egusi: pumpkin seeds, available shelled, either whole or ground. Egusi is used in West African cooking, providing a nutty texture to soups and stews.

Fish: flying fish, a distinctive 'winged' fish; king fish, a firm-fleshed 'meaty' fish, often sold as steaks; parrot fish, a brightly coloured fish with a beaky head; snapper, a popular, firm-fleshed fish, available in colours from grey to pinkish-red; trevalli, a large, firm-fleshed oily fish. Jacks is the name given to the smaller fish of the same family.

Gari: coarsely ground cassava, an African staple.

Guava: small, yellow-green, hard-skinned fruit with pinkish flesh filled with small seeds. It has a distinctive fragrance and is eaten raw or used to make jams and jellies.

Guinep: small, round, green fruit which grows in bunches. The pink flesh has a delicate flavour.

Irish moss: white, curly seaweed from which a drink of the same name is made. Available dried or in drink form.

Jackfruit: a large, green fruit with a pimply skin, similar in appearance to breadfruit.

Kenke: West African dumpling, made from fermented maize flour wrapped in corn husks or banana leaves and cooked.

Landsnails: giant snails, sold either alive, frozen, tinned or smoked. If bought alive keep them and feed them for a few days before cooking so they excrete anything toxic.

Mango: this large, kidney-shaped fruit, with its succulent orange flesh and sweet, resiny flavour, comes in numerous varieties. One of the best-known West Indian varieties is the Julie mango.

Okra (ladies' fingers, ochroes): finger-sized, ridged, tapering green pods, introduced into the Caribbean from West Africa.

Ortanique: a cross between an orange and a tangerine, this looks like an orange with a flattened end.

Palm hearts: tender palm tree hearts, usually found tinned.

Palm oil: a thick, orange-red oil, made from the fruit of the oil palm, which adds flavour and an orange colour to African dishes.

Pawpaw: long, oval fruit, with soft orange flesh, varying in skin-colour from green to orange.

Peppers: among the hottest and most flavourful of the peppers used in African and Caribbean cooking is the squat, rounded Scotch bonnet pepper, available in green, yellow and red varieties.

Pepper sauce: the sauce comes in a variety of textures from liquid to paste but is always hot!

Pigeon pea (gunga): ridged pea pods, with every pea in its own section. Unusually the peas within one pod vary in colour from cream through green and brown. Available fresh, tinned or dried.

Plaintain: similar in appearance to green bananas, plaintain have starchy flesh and are cooked and eaten as a vegetable. They can be chipped, boiled or cooked in stews.

Pomelo: often called shaddock, after the merchant ship captain who introduced the fruit to the Caribbean, this is a large, thick-skinned citrus fruit, similar in flavour to grapefruit.

Saltfish: preserved foods such as salted fish were brought over to the Caribbean to feed the plantation workers. It is now something of a luxury item. Stockfish is a popular salted fish.

Sapodilla (naseberry, chikoo): a fruit very similar in appearance to kiwi fruit, with a brown, furry skin. Inside it has pinky-brown, granular flesh with a few glossy pips and a distinctive sweet flavour.

Sorrel (rosella): the red sepals of a flowering plant, used either fresh or dried to make a dark red, aromatic drink, traditional at Christmas.

Soursop: a large, oval-shaped fruit with a thick, green, spiny skin. The pinkish-white flesh inside is custard-textured with a delicate, tart flavour.

Sugar cane: similar in appearance to bamboo, sugar cane has played a considerable part in Caribbean history as the sugar cane plantations needed extensive labour, provided by slaves. Short lengths of the woody stalk are sold to be chewed and sucked for their sweet refreshing juice.

Sweet potato: an edible sweet-fleshed tuber, available in many varieties.

Yam: a family of large, brown-skinned, starchy tubers, which come in many varieties, both yellow and white-fleshed.

AFRICAN & CARIBBEAN GLOSSARY

A TRIP TO AN ASIAN SUPERMARKET: NINE RECIPES

SPICED FRIED CASHEWS
SPICED FRUIT APPETISER
AUBERGINE FRITTERS
SAMAR'S SWEET AND SOUR PUMPKIN
VEGETABLE MUNG DAL
TINDOLA COUSCOUS
WHITE RADISH-STUFFED PARATHA
MANGO LASSI
MANGO IN CARDAMOM CUSTARD

Despite the fact that Indian restaurants are an everyday sight throughout British cities and towns, a trip to one of the larger Asian supermarkets reveals a number of unfamiliar ingredients which never appear on a standard curry-house menu. Most eye-catching is the array of Indian vegetables, from long skinny green drumsticks to knobbly-skinned bitter gourd or karela.

For the widest range of Asian food shops visit Ealing Road in Wembley, Southall Broadway or Upper Tooting Road. Here one finds large cash and carry stores in which to stock up your store-cupboard with spices, pulses, chutneys, flours and sacks of basmati rice, Indian greengrocers piled high with fruits and vegetables and sweetshops in which to buy a sustaining snack of samosas or burfi (a fudge-like Indian sweetmeat).

Ealing Road, Wembley

SPICED FRIED CASHEWS

Jumbo-sized bags of raw cashew nuts are a standard item in Asian supermarkets. Homemade fried cashew nuts are a traditional Indian nibble served with drinks.

Ingredients (serves four)

½ tsp ground cumin
½ tsp ground coriander
½ tsp salt
¼ tsp ground black pepper
¼ tsp chilli powder
oil for deep-frying
280 g/10 oz raw cashews

Mix together cumin, coriander, salt, black pepper and chilli powder.

Heat oil in a wok or karhai. Fry raw cashews in batches, frying until they darken to a deep golden brown. Remove with a slotted spoon to a shallow dish. Toss at once with spice mixture and set aside to cool.

SPICED FRUIT APPETISER

This colourful fruit dish, with a peppery chilli kick, makes a refreshing and unusual first course. Packets of chat masala (a particular spice mix) can be found in Asian food shops. The mixture of fruit can be varied, with papaya a popular element. Chikoo (sapodilla) look like smooth-skinned kiwi fruit or brown-skinned potatoes. Despite this nondescript appearance, however, they have delicious sweet pinky-brown flesh.

Ingredients (serves four)

2 bananas
2 oranges
juice of 1 lime
1 mango
3 chikoo
2 tsp of chat masala

Chikoo

Peel bananas and orange and slice into small chunks. Place in serving dish and toss with lime juice to prevent banana discolouring.

Slice mango cheeks off the large central stone. Turn each mango cheek flesh-side up and score with a criss-cross pattern, cutting the flesh into small cubes. Cut the mango cubes from the skin. (This leaves you with a large mango stone from which to suck the flesh – cook's perk!).

Peel the chikoo, slice in half lengthwise and remove the large glossy pips. Cut into chunks.

Add mango and chikoo to the serving dish, mixing well with banana and orange. Sprinkle over chat masala and mix well. Serve at once.

AUBERGINE FRITTERS

These tasty deep-fried fritters are known as pakoras and a whole assortment of fillings, from chicken pieces to whole chillies, can be used. The batter is made from cream-coloured chickpea flour, called gram flour or besan, and flavoured with lovage (ajwain or carom) seeds. Both ingredients can be found in Asian supermarkets. Serve the fritters with a zingy fresh coriander chutney.

Ingredients (feeds six to eight as an appetiser)

450 g/1 lb aubergines (preferably long slender ones)
salt
115 g/4 oz gram flour (besan)
1 tsp lovage (ajwain or carom) seeds
½ tsp cayenne pepper
150 ml/5 fl oz water
oil for deep frying

Slice the aubergines into 1 cm/½ in thick rounds. Sprinkle with salt and set aside for 20 minutes to draw out the bitter juices. Rinse and pat dry.

Meanwhile, make the batter. Sift gram flour into a mixing bowl. Mix in 1 tsp salt, lovage seeds and cayenne pepper. Gradually beat in water making a thick, smooth batter.

Heat oil in a wok or karhai. Test the heat by sprinkling in a few drops of batter. If they rise immediately to the surface then it's hot enough to start frying the fritters.

Fry the fritters in batches. Dip a few aubergine slices in the batter then add to the oil. Fry, turning over once, until a deep golden-brown on both sides. Remove with a slotted spoon and drain on kitchen paper. Serve while warm.

SAMAR'S SWEET AND SOUR PUMPKIN

Samar Manzoor has a devoted following addicted to her freshly-ground curry spice blends which she supplies mail-order through her company Samarkand (P.O. Box 12802, London NW3 3WJ, 0171-586 4809). Wonderfully aromatic and flavourful, her spice blends provide an insight into the range and diversity of authentic Indian cooking.

This dish is very much a family recipe and transforms the humble pumpkin (a shamefully neglected vegetable in English cookery) into a delicious curry. Dark brown tamarind pulp is used to add a sour note, while the sweetness comes from jaggery (soft orange-brown sugar made from palm or sugar cane). If these are unavailable Samar suggests substituting 1 tbsp of lime juice and 1 tbsp of honey instead and also points out that the levels of sweetness and sourness can be adjusted according to personal taste.

Ingredients
(serves two as a main course or four as a side-dish)

2 tbsp tamarind pulp	**Spice blend**
1.5 kg/3 lb 5 oz pumpkin	
1 onion	1½ tsp cumin
3 cloves garlic	1 tsp cayenne pepper
6 tbsp vegetable oil	1 tsp salt
200 g/7 oz tinned chopped tomato	1 tsp nigella
50 ml/ 2 fl oz water	¼ tsp turmeric
1½ tbsp jaggery	

Pour 4 tbsp hot water over the tamarind pulp. Set aside for 20 minutes. Mix thoroughly to extract as much of the pulp as possible. Strain through a sieve. Discard pulp and retain the brown tamarind water.

Meanwhle, peel the pumpkin and cut into 1 cm/½ in cubes. Peel and finely chop the onion. Peel and mince the garlic. Mix the spices together.

Heat the oil in a large saucepan. Add the onion and fry until it turns pale gold. Mix in the garlic and cook briefly.

Add in the chopped tomatoes, water, pumpkin and spice blend. Mix well.

Cook covered over a low heat for 20-25 minutes until the pumpkin is tender. Mix in the jaggery and tamarind, stirring until jaggery is melted. If there is any liquid in the pan increase the heat to medium to let it boil away.

VEGETABLE MUNG DAL

D als – the Hindi term for pulses – are a great Asian staple, used in a huge variety of dishes. Here small split yellow mung beans (mung dal, sometimes spelt moong dal), vegetables and spices make a thick soupy lentil dish. Packets of small curry leaves still on their stems are sold fresh or dried. Like bay leaves, curry leaves are used to add a distinctive flavour (in their case a slightly tart spiciness) but not eaten in their own right.

Ingredients (serves four)

175 g/6 oz mung dal (split yellow mung beans)
1.2 ltr/2 pt water
½ tsp salt
½ tsp ground turmeric
3 courgettes
175 g/6 oz green beans
2 garlic cloves
10 curry leaves
1 tbsp ghee/vegetable oil
2 tsp black mustard seeds
1 tsp cumin seeds

Ghee

Rinse the dal several times in cold water. Place in a large saucepan and add in 1.2 ltr/2 pts water, salt and turmeric. Bring to the boil, reduce heat, partly cover and simmer gently for 30 minutes, stirring occasionally.

Meanwhile, cut courgettes into 1 cm/½ in slices. Sprinkle with salt and set aside for 20 minutes to draw out bitter juices. Rinse, drain and pat dry

Top and tail green beans. Peel and roughly chop garlic.

When the dal has simmered for 30 minutes add in the courgette slices, green beans and curry leaves. Simmer for a further 30 minutes, stirring gently now and then.

Just before serving heat the ghee in a small frying pan. Add the black mustard seeds. A few seconds later when the mustard seeds begin to pop, add the cumin and garlic. Fry until garlic is browned then pour all the contents of the frying pan into the dal. Stir in and serve at once.

TINDOLA COUSCOUS

A mong the host of exotic-looking vegetables on sale in Asian greengrocers but rarely found elsewhere are several members of the squash family. Among these tiny walnut-sized tindola (tindori) - dark green with flecks of light green - are easy to spot. They have a refreshing flavour and are filled with small juicy edible seeds which gives them a crunchy texture.

This recipe combines tindola with carrot and soft-fleshed pumpkin in a traditional couscous recipe. The resulting medley of colours (green, orange and red) and textures is a pleasing one.

Ingredients (serves six)

2 onions
1 lb/450 g pumpkin
2 carrots
1 lb/450 g tindola (tindori or ivy gourd)
salt and freshly ground pepper
2 tbsp oil
1 tsp paprika
1 tsp ground cinnamon
¼ tsp ground saffron
400 g tin chopped tomatoes
300 ml/½ pt water
1 bunch coriander

Couscous

500 g/1 lb 2 oz couscous
600 ml/1 pt water
25 g/1 oz butter
salt

Peel and chop onions. Peel pumpkin and cut into 2.5 cm/1 in cubes. Peel carrots, halve lengthwise and cut into 2.5 cm/1 in lengths. Cut stems from tindola, slice in half lengthwise, sprinkle with salt and set aside for 30 mins to draw out juices.

Meanwhile, start cooking the vegetable stew. Heat oil in a casserole dish or large saucepan. Gently fry onion for 10 minutes. Mix in the paprika, cinnamon and saffron. Add in chopped tomatoes and water. Bring to the boil. Add in chopped pumpkin and carrot. Season with salt and freshly ground pepper. Reduce heat, cover and simmer gently for 20 minutes. Rinse the salted tindola and add to the vegetable stew. Simmer covered for a further 30 minutes.

While the tindola are cooking prepare the couscous. Place the couscous in a large bowl and pour over the water. Leave for 10 minutes until the water absorbed. Fluff the couscous with your fingers, breaking up any lumps. Melt the butter and mix in. Season with salt. Transfer couscous to a greased heatproof serving dish. Cover tightly with foil and heat through in the oven at Gas Mark 4/350F/180C for 20 minutes.

Rinse and finely chop the coriander. Stir into tindola stew. Serve couscous with tindola stew.

Tindola

WHITE RADISH-STUFFED PARATHA

Huge, long carrot-shaped white radish called mooli are another vegetable easily found in Asian supermarkets but rarely on an Indian restaurant menu. In this recipe they are used to add a slightly peppery savouriness to paratha, a classic Indian unleavened bread.

Ingredients (makes six parathas)

225 g/8 oz wholewheat flour
salt
150 ml/5 fl oz water
225 g/½ lb white radish (mooli)
1 onion
½ tbsp oil
1 tsp ground cumin
1 tsp ground coriander
3 tsp ghee

Mooli

Mix flour and 1 tsp salt in a large mixing bowl. Gradually add in the water, mixing in to make a soft dough. Knead for 8-10 minutes. Cover with a damp cloth and set aside for 1 hour.

Meanwhile, peel and grate the white radish. Wrap grated radish in a piece of muslin and squeeze several times to remove excess moisture. Peel and finely chop onion. Gently fry onion in oil until softened. Mix in cumin and coriander. Season to taste with salt. Mix fried onion with grated white radish.

Divide dough into six balls. Roll out the ball of dough on a lightly floured surface into a 10 cm/4 in circle. Place a tbsp of the white radish mixture in the centre of the dough circle. Fold the edges of the circle over the dough, sealing edges firmly. Roll out making an 18 cm/7 in circle. Repeat process making six stuffed parathas in all.

Heat a griddle or thick frying pan or tava. Brush one side of a paratha with ½ tsp of ghee. Cook ghee-side down on the hot griddle for 2-3 minutes, pressing down the edges with a spatula. Brush ½ tsp of ghee on the top side of the paratha then turn over and cook for a further 2-3 minutes. Both sides of the paratha should be flecked with brown-red patches. Remove and repeat process with remaining parathas. Serve parathas warm from the griddle.

MANGO LASSI

ASIAN

I f the only mango you've ever tried has been a rock-hard speciman from a Western supermarket then you haven't discovered the full joys of this much-prized tropical fruit. From late May to mid-August Asian supermarkets stock an abundance of mangoes, often at very reasonable prices. There are numerous mango varieties, with Alphonso, Honey and Kesar particularly prized. If you're lucky enough to have a glut of ripe mangoes then here are two recipes. The first is for a rich traditional Indian yogurt drink, the second for an elegant dessert, a delectable end to an Indian meal.

Ingredients (makes two glasses)

2 mangoes
200 g/7 oz Greek yogurt
125 ml/4 fl oz water

Slice the two mango cheeks off the large central stone. Scoop out the mango flesh. Rather than trying to scrape the flesh off the stone treat yourself and eat it yourself!

Place mango flesh (and any juice), yogurt and water in a blender. Process briefly until smooth. Pour into glasses and serve.

Mangoes

MANGO IN CARDAMOM CUSTARD

Ingredients (serves four)

600 ml/1 pt full fat milk
1 vanilla pod
3 cardamom pods
2 egg yolks
75 g/3 oz vanilla sugar
4 mangoes

Heat milk, vanilla pod and cardamom pods in a saucepan and bring to boiling point. Meanwhile, whisk together yolks and vanilla sugar in a large, heatproof bowl. Gradually pour in scalding milk, mixing well as you do so.

Return the milk mixture to the rinsed-out saucepan. Heat gently, stirring constantly, until slightly thickened. Remove from heat, transfer to a bowl, cover, cool and chill overnight or for at least 6 hours. Strain cardamom custard into a serving dish.

Take one of the mangoes and slice the mango cheeks off the large central stone. Turn each mango cheek flesh-side up and score with a criss-cross pattern, cutting the flesh into large cubes. Cut the mango cubes from the skin. Repeat process with each of the mangoes. Add the mango cubes to the cardamom custard and serve.

RECOMMENDED COOKBOOKS

Classic Indian Cooking,
Julie Sahni.
Authoritative, readable and usable.

Classic Indian Vegetarian Cooking,
Julie Sahni.
A truly inspiring book, elegantly written and filled with wonderful vegetarian recipes, from fritters to chutneys.

Fifty Great Curries of India,
Camellia Panjabi.
Mouthwateringly illustrated with full-page colour photographs , this authoritative book really does make you want to cook its recipes.

Madhur Jaffrey's Indian Cookery.
A very accessible, clearly-written introduction to Indian cuisine.

ASIAN GLOSSARY

Bitter gourd (karela): a knobbly-skinned, cucumber-shaped green gourd with a distinctive bitter flavour and digestive properties.

Bottle gourd (dudi): a large, smooth, bottle-shaped, green-skinned gourd with marrow-like flesh.

Cardamom: a fragrant spice pod sold whole, hulled and ready-ground. The small green or white cardamoms are used in both sweet and savoury dishes while the larger wrinkled black cardamom is used only in savoury dishes.

Carom (ajwan, lovage): a tiny seed spice, like miniature fennel seeds, with a medicinal scent and sharp, thyme-like flavour.

Chick–pea flour (gram or besan): ground chickpeas are the basis for many breads and fritters. Madhur Jaffrey recommends storing it in the fridge.

Chikoo (sapodilla): similar in appearance to kiwi fruit with a fine brown, furry skin, pinky-brown granular flesh, a few glossy pips and a distinctive sweet flavour.

Chilli powder: a hot red powder made from ground, dried red chillies.

Cluster beans (guar): fine, straight green beans.

Coconut milk: a thick white liquid made from grated coconut flesh and not, as is sometimes thought, from the cloudy liquid inside the coconut which is called `coconut water'. Homemade coconut milk can be made by blending together dessicated coconut with hot water then sieving it. Alternately tinned coconut milk is a convenient, ready-to-use product and Madhur Jaffrey recommends the Chaokoh brand. Creamed coconut or coconut milk powder need diluting before use.

Coriander: both the aromatic green leaves (similar in appearance to flat-leafed parsley) and small rounded seeds are used extensively in Indian cookery.

Cumin: small, greenish, finely-ridged oval seeds, similar to caraway seeds, with a distinctive, slightly sharp flavour, widely used in Indian cookery. Black cumin, which is rarer, has a more pronounced herbal flavour.

Curry leaf: a spicy-smelling leaf which resembles a small bay leaf. It's usually sold dried but sometimes branches of fresh curry leaves are available.

Dal: a term covering the three types of pulses (lentils, beans and peas) used in Indian cookery: chana dal, small yellow split peas; masoor dal, tiny pink split lentils (sometimes called red split lentils); moong dal, yellow split mung beans, sold both skinned and unskinned; rajma dal, red kidney beans; toovar dal, a large split yellow pea; urad dal, ivory-coloured hulled black gram beans, used in Southern Indian vegetarian cookery in dishes such as pancakes and fried dumplings.

Fennel: aniseed-flavoured, greenish ridged seeds, valued as a digestive. Candied fennel seeds are eaten after a meal.

Fenugreek (methi): both the small, stubby, hard, yellow seeds and the spicy-smelling, bitter green leaves are used in Indian cookery. The seeds have a strong, bitter flavour and are used in pickles. The dark green trefoil leaves, which look similar to clover, are sold both fresh and dried.

Fish: hilsa, a prized freshwater fish from Bangladesh; pomfret, a flat, round-shaped white-fleshed fish.

Garam masala: a fragrant spice mix available in many versions.

Ghee: clarified butter with a nutty flavour. Because of the clarification ghee can be used for deep frying and stored at room temperature.

Jackfruit: a huge fruit with a thick, green studded skin. The creamy-textured flesh inside is eaten as a vegetable when unripe and as a fruit when ripe.

Jaggery: a pale brown sugar with a rich, nutty flavour, made from sugar cane juice or palm sap and used in Indian sweets.

Mango: a kidney-shaped fruit, with succulent orange flesh and a sweet, resiny flavour, which is enormously popular in India. Tart, green unripe mangoes are used to make pickles, chutneys and relishes while orange-red ripe mangoes are eaten on their own and used in desserts. Over a thousand varieties are grown in India but the Alphonso mango is one of the best known over here.

Mustard oil: a pungent yellow oil, made from mustard seeds, used extensively in northern India and Bangladesh.

Mustard seeds: tiny, black round seeds, often used in pickles.

Okra (bhindi, ladies' fingers): a tapering, ridged green pod which exudes a sticky juice when cooked.

Onion seed (kalonji or nigella): tiny tear-shaped black seeds which, despite their name, are not related to onions. Used primarily in pickles but also on tandoori naan bread.

Panch phoran: a Bengali five-spice mix, containing cumin, fennel, onion seeds, fenugreek and black mustard seeds.

Pistachio: green-fleshed, delicately-flavoured nuts, used in Indian sweetmeats and ice-cream or as a nibble.

Poppy seed (khas khas): minuscule white poppy seeds, used in ground form to thicken sauces.

Rose essence: a delicate rose-scented essence used in desserts. Rose water is a diluted form of rose essence.

Saffron: the dried stigmas of a crocus variety, sold in both thread and powdered form.

Tamarind: a brown fleshy pod with a sour-sweet flavour, used as a souring agent. Both tamarind pulp and tamarind paste are available.

Tindola (tindori): walnut-sized ivy gourds with variegated markings and a crisp, crunchy texture.

Turmeric (haldi): a small-fingered, orange-fleshed rhizome from which comes the powdered yellow spice powder of the same name.

White radish (mooli): long, thick white radish, with a mild flavour, used to stuff parathas in Pakistani cooking.

Yard-long beans: exceedingly long, thin green beans.

Yogurt: traditionally made from buffalo's milk, Julie Sahni suggests stirring a little soured cream into normal yogurt to reproduce the necessary tangy flavour.

ASIAN GLOSSARY

A TRIP TO CHINATOWN: TEN RECIPES

CHICKEN CHIVE WONTON PARCELS
CHAR KWAY TEOW
LYDIA'S CHICKEN CLAY POT CASSEROLE
VEGETARIAN SPRING ROLLS
UNCLE KIM'S LAKSA
HUNG SUI TOFU
ROJAK
CONSTANT'S SUMMER CHICKEN
BLACK BEAN WATER SPINACH
ALMOND JELLY WITH LONGANS

'm always amazed at the range of ingredients even the smallest Chinese supermarket manages to squeeze on to its shelves. As one strolls through Gerrard Street it is the array of fresh fruits and vegetables on display outside the shops which is particularly eye-catching: bundles of fresh green vegetables such as bok choy, gai laan, choi sum and purple-hearted Chinese spinach and fruits including string bags of red-shelled lychees, mangoes and tiny orange kumquats. Shop workers stand outside deftly sorting through, trimming and bundling up the vegetables. The Golden Gate Grocers (0171-437 6266) at 16 Newport Place, WC2 always has a good selection of fresh produce, most of it helpfully labelled in English.

In the summer months a host of tropical fruit can be found: hairy rambutans, dark purple mangosteens and, most spectacularly, huge spiky durians with their rich, all-pervasive odour. The Chinese shops have always acted as umbrella suppliers for South East Asian provisions with Thai ingredients increasingly available in Chinatown so I have included a few South East Asian dishes in this chapter.

Chinatown

CHICKEN CHIVE WONTON PARCELS

L ong dark green Chinese chives have a powerful flavour more akin to wild garlic than our delicate chives and give these appetising nibbles a distinctive taste. Wonton wrappers, little squares of yellow dough, are sold pre-packed in the chilled cabinet.

Ingredients (makes 28)

1 chicken breast fillet (approx 140 g/5 oz)
1 cm/½ in root ginger
25 g/1 oz Chinese chives
oil for deep-frying
1 tbsp soy sauce
28 wonton wrappers
1 egg white

Dipping sauce

2 tbsp chilli sauce/sambal
juice of ½ lime

Chinese Chives

Mince or finely chop the chicken, quickly done in a food processor if you have one. Peel and finely chop root ginger. Finely chop Chinese chives.

Heat 1 tbsp of the oil in a frying pan. Fry minced chicken until whitened. Remove with a slotted spoon. Mix in ginger, Chinese chives and soy sauce and set aside to cool.

Take one wonton wrapper. Place ½ tsp of the chicken mixture in the centre of the wrapper. Lightly brush the wrapper edges with egg white. Fold the wrapper over the chicken to form a triangular parcel, sealing the edges firmly. Repeat the process until all the wrappers are filled.

Mix together the chilli sauce and lime juice.

Heat the oil in a wok until very hot. Deep-fry the wonton parcels in small batches. Providing the oil is hot enough they should puff up immediately, expanding in size, and turning deep gold. Turn the wrappers over to cook briefly on the other side then remove with a slotted spoon. Drain on kitchen paper.

Serve as soon as possible with the chilli dipping sauce.

CHAR KWAY TEOW

My version of a classic South East Asian 'hawker' dish freshly made to order by street food vendors or hawkers. The broad flat fresh rice noodles, found pre-packed in plastic bags near the chilled section, give the dish a special slippery texture. Lap cheong sausages resemble small, narrow fatty salamis (but unlike salami must be cooked before eating) and are sold both vacuum-packed or loose, hanging from large wire hooks. Bok choy is a green leafy vegetable with distinctive white stems.

Ingredients (serves four)

450 g/1 lb fresh rice noodles (ho fun)
2 cloves garlic
2 lap cheong sausages
115 g/4 oz bok choy leaves
1 red chilli
2 eggs
1 lime
3 tbsp groundnut/sunflower oil
115 g/4 oz cooked peeled prawns
1 tsp sugar
2 tbsp oyster sauce
2 tbsp dark soy sauce
115 g/4 oz bean sprouts

Lap Cheong Sausages

Place the noodles in a colander and pour over a kettleful of just-boiled water, stirring the noodles with a chopstick as you do so. Chop the softened noodles into short lengths.

Peel and chop garlic. Finely slice the lap cheong sausages. Shred the bok choy. Chop the chilli, discarding stem. Beat the eggs. Quarter the lime.

Heat the oil in a wok. Fry the lap cheong sausage until slightly browned. Add the garlic and chilli and fry until garlic is golden-brown. Add in noodles, bok choy and prawns, mixing well. Add in sugar, oyster sauce and soy sauce. Stir-fry for 3 minutes. Add the bean sprouts and fry until just wilted. Pour in the egg and mix in with the noodles, frying until the cooked egg flecks the noodles. Serve at once.

LYDIA'S CHICKEN CLAY POT CASSEROLE

Born in Singapore my mother Lydia Linford has now lived in London for many years. She is an inventive cook, improvising with a large range of ingredients. As a small child I would tag along after her on food shopping trips to Soho visiting Italian delis and Chinese supermarkets – outings that underlie my Gastro-Soho Tours.

When cooking during the week after work she tends to opt for simple pasta dishes, either Italian or Chinese-style. When entertaining friends and family, however, she goes to great lengths, shopping days in advance for special ingredients and preparing a true feast.

The dried Chinese black mushrooms give this homely dish a rich distinctive flavour. Clay pots are sold in Chinese supermarkets and are ideal for slow-cooked braised dishes but a good casserole dish is an excellent substitute. Lydia suggests serving this with steamed rice, a leafy green vegetable and a steamed or baked Chinese fish dish.

Ingredients (serves four as part of a Chinese meal)

400 g/14 oz chicken breast with skin on
2 in/5 cm piece of root ginger
3 tbsp rice wine/medium dry sherry
1 tbsp sesame oil
3 tbsp dark soy sauce
1 tsp cornflour
8 large dried Chinese black mushrooms
150 g/5 oz tinned bamboo shoot chunks

2 spring onions
3 shallots
4 cloves garlic
2 tbsp groundnut/sunflower oil
1 tsp sugar
salt and pepper

Cut chicken into small chunks. Cut the ginger in half and peel and grate one of the pieces. Mix together rice wine, sesame oil, soy sauce, grated ginger and cornflour. Mix in the chicken pieces, cover and marinate in the fridge for at least 30 minutes.

Pour 300ml/½pt warm water over the dried mushrooms and set aside to soak for 30 minutes. Remove mushrooms but do not discard mushroom water. Cut stems off soaked mushrooms and discard. Squeeze mushroom caps dry and cut into halves.

Cut bamboo shoots into wedges. Slice spring onions in half lengthwise then cut diagonally into 2.5 cm/1 in lengths. Peel and slice shallots. Peel and crush garlic. Peel and finely chop remaining root ginger.

Heat the oil in a wok. Over medium heat saute the garlic, shallots and ginger until fragrant. Add the chicken pieces (reserving marinade) and fry until browned.

Mix in the sliced mushrooms, bamboo shoots, sugar, chicken marinade and strained mushroom water.

Transfer the chicken mixture to a hotpot or small casserole dish.

Bake in the oven at Gas Mark 4/350F/180C for 50 minutes. Season to taste with salt and pepper. Sprinkle over the spring onion lengths and serve at once.

CHINESE

Clay Pots

35

VEGETARIAN SPRING ROLLS

Making your own spring rolls allows you to be inventive (and generous) with the filling. This recipe uses cellophane noodles, fine glossy white noodles made from mung bean starch. In their dried state these noodles are extremely tough. Upon soaking they soften enough to be cut and become translucent in the process, as their name suggests. Packets of spring roll wrappers can be found either in the chilled section or the freezer.

Ingredients (makes 20)

115 g/4 oz cellophane noodles
6 dried Chinese black mushrooms
2 cloves garlic
2.5 cm/1 in piece of root ginger
2 spring onions
175 g/6 oz green beans
25 g/1 oz fresh coriander
groundnut oil for deep-frying
2 tbsp medium dry sherry
1 tsp sesame oil
2 tbsp thin soy sauce
115 g/4 oz fresh beansprouts
1 egg white
20 spring roll wrappers (21 cm x 21 cm), thoroughly thawed if frozen

Pour boiling water over cellophane noodles and leave to soak for 20 minutes. Drain and cut noodles into short lengths.

Meanwhile, in a separate bowl, pour boiling water over Chinese mushrooms and leave to soak for 20 minutes. Drain, cut off and discard stems, squeeze dry and finely shred.

Peel and finely chop garlic and root ginger. Trim and finely chop spring onion. Top and tail green beans. Slice into short fine strips. Finely chop fresh coriander.

Heat wok. Add in 2 tbsp of the oil. Fry garlic and ginger until fragrant. Add in green beans and mushroom shreds. Stir-fry briefly. Add in cellophane noodles, spring onion and bean sprouts. Stir-fry for 2 minutes. Pour in sherry, sesame oil and soy sauce. Stir-fry mixing well for 3 minutes. Transfer noodle mixture to a dish and mix in coriander. Set aside to cool.

When the noodle mixture has cooled make the spring rolls. Like filo pastry, spring roll wrappers dry out and become brittle very quickly. To prevent this cover the opened packet of wrappers with a dampened clean tea towel and take the wrappers out one at a time.

Place a spring roll wrapper on a plate so that it forms a diamond shape. Place 2 tbsp of the filling slightly below the centre. Fold the bottom corner of the wrapper up over the filling. Start to tightly roll up the wrapper, folding in the two side flaps. Brush the final corner flap with egg white and press it down tightly round the spring roll. Repeat the process making 20 spring rolls.

Heat the oil in a wok until very hot. Fry the spring rolls in batches of three to four until they are golden-brown all over, turning over once in the process. Remove with a slotted spoon, drain on kitchen paper and serve while hot.

CHINESE

Root Ginger

UNCLE KIM'S LAKSA

Laksa is a rich spicy Malay coconut milk soup with noodles and fish balls, substantial enough to be a meal in its own right rather than a first course. This recipe is based on one given to me by my Singaporean uncle Kim Bong on a recent family visit.

Aromatic galingale, which looks like a white-pink version of root ginger, and lemon grass are often stored in chilled cabinets.

Packets of ready-made fish balls and thick white fresh beehoon noodles can be found in the chilled cabinets.

Both the blachan (shrimp paste) and dried shrimps have a strong fishy odour (one which sends my cat into an ecstatic sniffing prowl round the kitchen!) and should be stored in airtight containers.

Ingredients (serves four)

75 g/3 oz dried shrimps
2 small onions
4 cloves garlic
5 cm/2 in piece of galingale
3 stalks lemon grass
1 tsp blachan (dried shrimp paste)
1 tsp ground turmeric
1 tsp ground chilli
4 tsp ground coriander
½ lb/225 g beansprouts
450 g/1 lb beehoon noodles
½ cucumber
2 tbsp oil
2 x 400 ml tins coconut milk
200 g/7 oz small white fish balls
8 raw peeled tiger prawns
salt

Finely grind the dried shrimps and set aside.

Peel and finely chop onions, garlic and galingale. Remove tough outer leaves and finely chop the lower white bulbous part of the lemon grass stalks. Blend together onion, garlic, galingale, lemon grass, blachan, turmeric, chilli and coriander into a paste.

Blanch the beansprouts. Wash the beehoon noodles. Cover with boiling water to soften them, then drain. Peel cucumber and cut into short fine strips. Divide the noodles and beansprouts among four deep serving bowls.

Heat the oil in a large saucepan. Fry the onion paste for five minutes until fragrant. Mix in the coconut milk and, stirring, bring to the boil. Stir in the ground dried shrimps, fish balls and tiger prawns. Simmer gently until fish balls are heated through and prawns cooked. Add salt to taste.

Pour coconut soup over the noodles and beansprouts. Top with cucumber shreds and serve at once.

HUNG SUI TOFU

This recipe was kindly given to me by Mrs Wong and her daughters Juliana and Vera, with whom it's a family favourite. Fresh tofu (beancurd) can be found in the chilled sections of Chinese supermarkets, packed in water in sealed containers. With its delicate flavour and texture it is a world away from the stolid long-life beancurd sold in Western supermarkets and should be eaten within a day of purchase.

Vera suggests serving this quick and tasty beancurd dish with rice or noodles.

Ingredients
(serves one or two as a main dish, two to four if accompanying other dishes)

600 g pkt fresh white tofu (beancurd)
2-3 cloves garlic
3 spring onions
1 tsp cornflour
3 tbsp groundnut/sunflower oil
a pinch of salt
2 tbsp yellow bean sauce
½ tsp sugar

Carefully slice tofu into 16 even-sized cubes. Peel and finely chop garlic. Cut spring onion (green and white parts) into 2.5 cm/1 in sections. Mix cornflour with 6 tbsp water.

Heat wok until very hot. Add oil and a pinch of salt. Add garlic and fry until browned. Add tofu cubes and brown on each side for 1 minute. Add in yellow bean sauce and sugar. Stir-fry for 1 minute. Pour in cornflour paste. Stir-fry for 1 minute. Remove from heat. Mix in spring onions and serve at once.

ROJAK

This is a delicious salad, tossed in a thick chilli-hot salty sweet sauce. The saltiness comes both from blachan (dried shrimp paste sold in packets) and thick, sticky prawn paste (petis udang) sold in small plastic jars. Brown tamarind pulp adds a faint sourness while gula melaka (palm sugar sold in cylindrical blocks) gives a fudgy sweetness.

The salad ingredients include deep-fried beancurd (spongy, golden-brown cubes sold in packets and found in the chilled section) and yambean (jicama). The latter is a tuber which looks like a large, pale brown turnip and its crunchy dense white flesh tastes like a cross between an apple and a turnip.

Ingredients (serves six)

1 tsp blachan (dried shrimp paste)
2 red chillies
55 g/2 oz salted roasted peanuts
1 tbsp tamarind pulp
55 g/2 oz gula melaka sugar
1 tbsp prawn paste
juice of ½ lime
1 yambean (approx 225 g/8 oz)
½ cucumber
225 g/8 oz deep-fried beancurd
1 small pineapple
225 g/8 oz beansprouts

Dry-fry the blachan for 2-3 minutes on each side. De-stem and pound red chillies. Finely grind peanuts. Pour 50 ml/2 fl oz warm water over tamarind pulp and leave to stand for a few minutes. Stir well, then strain.

Crumble the gula melaka into small pieces. Pour over the tamarind water and stir until sugar is dissolved.

Mix together the blachan, pounded chilli and prawn paste. Mix in the tamarind sugar syrup, lime juice and ground peanuts.

Peel the yambean and cut into small chunks. Slice cucumber into ½ cm/¼ in thick pieces. Halve beancurd squares. Trim pineapple and cut into small chunks. Blanch and drain beansprouts. Mix yambean, cucumber, beancurd, pineapple and beansprouts in serving dish. Pour over peanut sauce, mix thoroughly and serve.

CHINESE

CONSTANT'S SUMMER CHICKEN

When Constant Leung first arrived in London from Hong Kong in the '60s, Chinatown was the only place in which to buy Chinese ingredients. Now, however, most basic Chinese ingredients are readily available in his local supermarket. Constant, however, stocks up with more specialist ingredients such as Chinese rice wine or good soy sauce when he eats out in Chinatown. A keen and experimental cook, he has an eye for the details by which a dish succeeds or fails.

The spice star anise adds a delicate liquorice flavour to the chicken in this traditional Cantonese dish. In these days of bland factory-farmed chicken it's important to use the best chicken you can. Constant strongly recommends using corn-fed chicken for a good result.

Constant suggests serving this with plain boiled Thai fragrant rice and stir-fried mangetout.

Ingredients (serves four)

a corn-fed chicken (approx 1.3 kg/3 lb)
1 star anise
14 spring onions
175 g/6 oz root ginger
salt and freshy ground pepper
1 lollo rosso lettuce
8 tbsp corn oil
a few sprigs of coriander, to garnish

Half-fill a large saucepan (large enough to hold the chicken in) with water and bring to the boil. Put the chicken and the star anise into the boiling water (which should cover the chicken), reduce heat and boil gently for 20-25 minutes uncovered until cooked. To test whether the chicken is cooked Constant suggests inserting a knife or chopstick into the thickest part of the chicken. If it is cooked the insertion and withdrawal should be effortless and there should be no sign of rawness.

Remove the chicken from the saucepan and set aside to cool for at least 30 minutes.

Trim spring onions and chop both white and green parts very finely. Peel and chop the root ginger extremely finely. This can be done with a food processor though Constant warns against turning the ginger into a paste. Mix together spring onion and root ginger in a heatproof container. Season with salt and pepper.

Separate the lollo rosso and wash and dry the leaves. Cut large leaves into small strips. Cover a large serving plate with the lollo rosso leaves.

When the chicken is cooled remove the skin. Cut off the breast meat and cut into bite-size chunks. Place the breast meat in the centre of the bed of lettuce. De-bone the rest of the chicken and cut the chickenmeat into bite-size chunks. Arrange these chunks round the breast meat, leaving a ring of lettuce around the edge of the serving dish.

Heat the corn oil in a pan until the top of the oil is smoking, being careful not to let it burn. Pour the hot oil over the spring onion and ginger mixture, where it will sizzle dramatically. Spread the spring onion mixture over the chickenmeat, garnish with coriander sprigs and serve.

BLACK BEAN WATER SPINACH

A number of leafy green vegetables play an important part in Chinese cooking. Among these is water spinach (ong choi or kang kong) which has long narrow green leaves and distinctive hollow stems. When cooked the leaves wilt quickly but the stems retain a certain crunchiness.

This quick and simple stir-fry dish uses black beans, fermented soya beans which add a distinctive rich flavour. These are sold in cans, usually labelled 'black beans in salted sauce'. Once opened transfer the remaining contents of the can to a sealed container and store in the fridge where they will keep indefinitely.

Serve as a vegetable side-dish with a Chinese meal.

Ingredients (serves four)

2 cloves garlic
450 g/1 lb water spinach (kang kong)
1½ tbsp black beans
2 tbsp peanut oil
1 tbsp thin soy sauce

Peel and roughly chop garlic. Rinse and roughly chop water spinach, discarding lowest 2.5 cm/1 in – 5 cm/2 in of the stems as these can be too tough. Rinse black beans in water to remove excess saltiness.

Heat wok. Add oil. Fry black beans and garlic until garlic turns golden. Add in water spinach. Stir-fry until just wilted. Add in soy sauce. Stir-fry for 1 minute. Serve at once.

ALMOND JELLY WITH LONGANS

This is a classic Chinese dessert combining cool cubes of almond jelly (resembling bean curd) with tinned longans, a slightly crunchier relation of lychees. The jelly is set with agar-agar, a setting agent derived from seaweed (useful to know about if you're avoiding gelatine on grounds of BSE). Agar-agar is sold in long crunchy strands (which look rather like crumpled plastic) or in powdered form.

Lychees can be substituted for longans. In either case this is a pleasantly light dessert, ideal for rounding off a Chinese meal.

Ingredients (serves four)

600 ml/1 pt water
5 g/ ⅛ oz agar-agar strands
3 tbsp sugar
150 ml/¼ pt evaporated milk
2 tsp almond essence
435 g tin longans in syrup

Bring water to the boil in a large saucepan. Mix in agar-agar strands. Reduce heat and simmer, stirring often, for 10-15 minutes until agar-agar is dissolved.

Stir in sugar and simmer stirring until dissolved. Pour in evaporated milk and gently stir in.

Strain through a fine sieve into a bowl. Stir in almond essence. Cool, cover and chill until set (around 1 hour). Cut into diamond-shaped lozenges. Transfer to a serving dish. Pour over longans and their syrup and serve.

RECOMMENDED COOKBOOKS

Chinese Cookery,
Ken Hom.
An accessible, basic introduction to Chinese cooking.

Classic Chinese Cookbook,
Yan-Kit So.
A wonderful book, filled with authentic-tasting, clearly written recipes and useful illustrations. Essential for anyone interested in Chinese cooking.

CHINESE GLOSSARY

Agar agar: a vegetarian setting agent obtained from seaweed which does not require refrigeration to set, available either in powdered form or translucent strands.

Bamboo shoots: fresh bamboo shoots are occasionally available. Tinned bamboo shoots, either whole or sliced, are easily found.

Bean curd (tofu): a soyabean product which has always been a valuable source of protein in Chinese cooking. Fresh ivory-coloured bean curd has a firm custard texture and bland flavour. It is sold in the chilled section, packed in water. Deep-fried bean curd has a golden colour and spongy texture and is found in packets in the chilled section. Bean curd 'cheese', either red or white, is fermented bean curd with a strong, salty taste and is sold in jars. Dried bean-curd sheets are sold in packets.

Beansprouts: white crispy sprouts of the mung bean; also available are the larger, nuttier soya bean sprouts, which should be cooked before eating.

Black beans: small black soya beans, fermented with salt and spices, with a pungent flavour.

Chilli oil: a transparent oil, tinted red from chillies, sold in small bottles and with a powerful chilli kick.

Chinese broccoli (gai laan): a thick-stalked vegetable with large rounded leaves and white flowers.

Chinese cabbage (bok choy): similar in appearance to Swiss chard, with dark green leaves and thick white stems. Green bok choy, with green leaves and stems, is also available.

Chinese chives: long, dark green, flat leaves, with a stronger and more pungent odour and flavour than English chives, also sold blanched and complete with buds.

Chinese cinnamon: cassia bark, sold in sticks similar to cinnamon but larger and rougher with a stronger flavour.

Chinese flowering cabbage (choi sum): a leafy vegetable with rounded leaves, small yellow flowers and long stems.

Chinese leaves: a large tight head of white-green crinkly leaves with a crunchy texture, widely available.

Chinese mushrooms: black, dried mushrooms with a distinctive meaty flavour. Prices vary according to the size and thickness of the caps.

Chinese sausages: these resemble small, fatty salamis, but must be cooked before eating. There are two sorts: pork and pork and liver, the latter being darker in colour. They are found in packets or hanging up in bunches with other dried meats.

Coriander: this green herb, similar in appearance to flat-leaved continental parsley but with a distinctive sharp flavour, is one of the few herbs used in Chinese cooking.

Five-spice powder: fragrant, golden-brown powder made from five or sometimes six ground spices, with the four base spices being star-anise, Chinese cinnamon, cloves and fennel seeds. Szechuan peppercorns, ginger and cardamom are the additions.

Ginger: an aromatic rhizome, available fresh in knobbly, light brown 'root' form.

Glutinous rice: rounded rice grains with a sticky texture when cooked, used in both sweet and savoury dishes.

Golden needles: long dried buds of the tiger-lily flower.

Longan: a small brown skinned fruit, related to the lychee, with translucent flesh and glossy black seed, also known as 'dragon's eye' fruit. Available either tinned or fresh.

Lotus leaves: the large leaves of the water-lily plant, available dried and used for wrapping food for cooking.

Lotus root: a crunchy root with a decorative tracery of holes, available fresh, in sausage-like links, or tinned.

Mooli: a large, long white radish, with crispy white flesh.

Mustard Greens (gaai choi): a green large-leafed plant. The bitter varieties are pickled rather than cooked.

Noodles: cellophane noodles (also known as beanthread, glass or transparent noodles) are fine threadlike noodles made from mung beans and need soaking before they can be easily cut; egg noodles, made from wheat flour, egg and water, are distinguished by their yellow colour; rice noodles and vermicelli, dried, white noodles of varying widths made from rice flour which need soaking before use; river rice noodles (sarhor noodles), made from ground rice and water, steamed in thin sheets and cut into strips. Fresh river rice noodles are sold in clear packets, usually stored near the chilled section.

Potato flour: fine white flour, made from cooked potatoes, used as a thickener.

Rice vinegar: mild vinegars ranging from delicate white rice vinegar to sweet red rice vinegar and rich black rice vinegar.

Rice wine: made from glutinous rice, yeast and water, this is used for both drinking and cooking.

Sauces: chilli bean sauce, a hot, spicy, dark sauce made from soya beans and chillies; chilli sauce, a bright red sweet chilli sauce; hoisin sauce, a thick, brown fruity sauce; oyster sauce, a thick, brown sauce made from oysters; soy sauce, a dark brown salty liquid made from fermented soya beans, available as thin, salty Light Soy Sauce or as thicker, sweeter Dark Soy Sauce; yellow bean sauce, a thick, brown sauce made from fermented yellow beans.

Sesame oil: a nutty, golden-coloured oil made from sesame seeds.

Shrimps, dried: small, shelled, dried pink shrimps, with a strong salty flavour.

Spring roll wrappers: white paper-thin wrappers, available in different sizes. Found in either the chilled or freezer sections.

Star-anise: dark brown, star-shaped pod with a distinctive licorice favour and scent.

Straw mushrooms: cone-shaped mushrooms, usually available canned.

Szechuan peppercorns: fragrant, reddish-brown 'peppercorns', the dried berries of a shrub.

Szechuan pickled vegetables: mustard green roots, pickled in salt and hot chillies, a speciality of Szechuan province.

Tangerine peel: in its dried form, in dark brown pieces, this is used as a flavouring in Chinese cooking.

Thousand-year-old eggs: preserved duck eggs, with a pungent flavour, which are in fact only about a hundred days old.

Water chestnuts: the crunchy bulbs of a waterplant. Fresh, brown-skinned bulbs are sometimes found, but tinned water chestnuts are easily available.

Water spinach (ong chai): a narrow-leafed plant with a mild, spinach-like flavour.

Winter melon: a large green gourd with white flesh, available whole or in pieces, and often used to make soup.

Wonton skins: small squares of yellow egg-noodle dough, used to wrap up dumplings. Found in either chilled or freezer sections.

Wood ears: black, crinkled, dried fungus with a beige underside.

CHINESE GLOSSARY

A TRIP TO A CYPRIOT GREENGROCER: SEVEN RECIPES

PINE NUT BULGAR PILAFF
MARIA'S DOLMADES (STUFFED VINE LEAVES)
CYPRIOT-STYLE BLACK-EYED BEANS
JULIA'S COLOCASSI WITH PORK
PURSLANE SALAD
PEACH FILO PARCELS
STELLA'S SEMOLINA CAKE

L iving as I do in Haringey means that I'm lucky enough to have a number of Greek Cypriot greengrocers within walking distance of my home, my favourite being Antonios Athanasiou's Continental Stores at 140, High Road, N2 (0181-444 5545) in East Finchley.

There's always a tempting range of good quality seasonal fruits and vegetables plus abundant bunches of fresh mint, flat-leafed parsley and dill. Cypriot produce is proudly labelled as such, from new potatoes to courgettes, and cooking tips handed out generously. Most Greek greengrocers also have a grocery section stocked with Greek staples and here one finds the essentials for Mediterranean cooking: olives, rosewater (used to flavour desserts), packets of semolina, bulgar wheat and pulses while the chilled section contains tubs of thick Greek yogurt, salty feta and halloumi cheese.

Continental Stores

PINE NUT BULGAR PILAFF

Bulgar wheat (or pourgouri or cracked wheat) gives this pilaff a pleasantly nutty flavour and slightly chewy texture. Because bulgar wheat has already been partly cooked it is very quick to cook and makes a delicious accompaniment to stews.

Ingredients (serves four)

1 onion
25 g/1 oz vermicelli
15 g/½ oz butter
1 tbsp olive oil
1 tbsp pine nuts
1 tsp ground cinnamon
250 g/9 oz bulgar wheat
400 ml/14 fl oz chicken stock
salt
2 tbsp chopped flat-leaf parsley

Peel and finely chop the onion. Break the vermicelli into short pieces.

Heat butter and olive oil in a heavy-bottomed saucepan. Add in onion and fry gently until softened. Mix in vermicelli and pine nuts and fry gently for a further 5 minutes.

Sprinkle over cinnamon and mix in well. Mix in bulgar. Pour in stock and season with salt. Bring to the boil. Reduce heat, cover tightly and simmer over a very low heat for 10 minutes until stock is absorbed. Transfer to a serving dish, sprinkle over chopped parsley and serve at once.

MARIA'S DOLMADES (STUFFED VINE LEAVES)

Maria and Petros Yiannoullou came from Cyprus to London after World War II. Petros worked here as a restaurateur for many years and the couple divide their time between London and Cyprus.

A keen gardener, Maria practically lives in her North London garden where she cultivates everything from fresh vine leaves to lahana (Swiss chard). When not in the garden she is in the kitchen where she cooks enough food to feed an army. Even a casual visitor to the Yiannoullou house is offered an assortment of home-baked biscuits and cakes. When she is back in Cyprus her family in London receive food parcels containing delicious Cypriot produce.

Dolmades or stuffed vine leaves are a classic Greek dish, delicious either hot or cold. Packets of vine leaves in brine are available all the year round but in the summer months look out for fresh vine leaves at Greek or Middle Eastern greengrocers.

Ingredients (serves four)

2 tbsp olive oil
450 g/1 lb minced lamb
225 g/8 oz long grain rice
1 onion
3 tomatoes
2 tbsp chopped parsley
2 tbsp chopped mint
salt and pepper
a 225 g/8 oz packet of vine leaves in brine
a few lettuce leaves
juice of 2 lemons
1 tbsp tomato puree

Mix the olive oil into the minced lamb. Wash the rice to rinse out excess starch. Peel and finely chop the onion. Finely dice the tomatoes. Mix together minced lamb, rice, onion, tomatoes, parsley and mint. Season well with salt and pepper.

Pour boiling water over the vine leaves, leave to soak for a minute or so, then drain – this removes the excess briny saltiness. If using fresh vine leaves simply scald very briefly in boiling water to soften them, drain and rinse in cold water. Cut the stems off the vine leaves.

Take one vine leaf and place it ridged side up. Place a tablespoon of the meat mixture in the centre of the leaf. Roll the leaf up tightly over the filling, folding it into a small cigar-shaped parcel (in fact the Cypriot name for dolmades 'koupepia' means little cigar).

Line a casserole dish with a layer of lettuce leaves to prevent the dolmades from burning. Tightly pack in the stuffed vine leaves in layers. Pour over water, tomato puree and lemon juice, adding enough liquid to just cover the vine leaves.

Press a plate down upon the vine leaves to hold them in place. Cover and cook gently over a low heat for around ½ hour.

CYPRIOT-STYLE BLACK-EYED BEANS

Fresh black-eyed beans (louvi) have long slender bumpy green pods. Michael Athanasiou, at my local greengrocer, gave me this traditional recipe combining louvi with Cypriot marrow (balcaba) which, just as he assured me, is sweeter and more flavourful than our English marrow. Simplicity itself, this dish allows the fresh flavours of the vegetables to come through.

Ingredients (serves four)

350 g/12 oz fresh black-eyed beans (louvi)
350 g/12 oz Cypriot marrow (balcaba)/marrow
salt and freshly ground pepper
juice of ½ lemon
1 tbsp olive oil

Top, tail and string the black-eyed beans and cut them into 5 cm/2 in lengths. Cut the marrow into small chunks.

Bring a large pan of salted water to the boil. Add in the beans. Cook them for 5 minutes then add in the marrow. Cook for a few minutes until marrow is just tender. Drain and toss with lemon juice and olive oil. Season with freshly ground pepper and serve at once.

JULIA'S COLOCASSI WITH PORK

When Julia Papantonis was a child in Cyprus her mother would cook this rich tasty stew for her and her brothers and sisters. Now this dish is a firm favourite with Julia's own family. Hospitable and sociable, Julia loves cooking and enjoys making the traditional Cypriot dishes such as melomakarouna, the meltingly sweet syrup-soaked biscuits which are a Christmas treat.

Colocassi, a Cypriot variety of taro, is easy to spot as it is a large brown-skinned tuber with a distinctive stump at one end. Once the colocassi has been peeled do not get it wet as it then becomes slimy. Julia recommends buying the colocassi in one piece as different pieces cook at different speeds.

Serve the stew with slices of Cypriot 'village bread', the large round flat loaves one sees in Greek shops.

Ingredients (serves four)

1 kg/2 lb 4 oz colocassi (bought in one piece)
1 onion
2 stalks of celery with leaves left on
2 potatoes
3 tbsp olive oil
500 g/1 lb 2 oz cubed pork
600 ml/1 pt passata (sieved tomatoes)
½ tsp ground cinnamon
600 ml/1 pt chicken stock
salt and freshly ground pepper

Wash and scrub the colocassi then dry it thoroughly. Peel and cut off the stump then chip off pieces of the colocassi.

Peel and finely chop the onion. Chop the celery. Quarter the potatoes.

Heat the oil in a casserole dish or large heavy-bottomed saucepan. Add in the cubed pork and brown on all sides. Remove the pork with a slotted spoon and set aside.

Add onion, celery and colocassi to the casserole dish and fry, stirring, until the onion is translucent. Mix in the passata and cinnamon, cook briefly then return the browned pork to the casserole dish. Keep stirring while adding in the stock. Season with salt and freshly ground pepper.

Cover and simmer gently for 45 minutes to 1 hour until the pork and colocassi are tender, stirring now and then.

PURSLANE SALAD

Purslane or glysterida is a salad leaf, one of the characteristic components of the Greek peasant salad known as horiatiki salata, made up from a seasonal mixture of vegetables.

Purslane has fleshy stalks and small rounded leaves, rather like large clover leaves, and a fresh, tangy lemony taste. Rather extravagantly one uses the young tips, discarding the remaining tough stems.

Ingredients (serves four as a side-salad)

225 g/½ lb purslane (glysterida)
1 baby cucumber
2 tomatoes
1 spring onion
3 oz/75 g feta cheese
3 tbsp olive oil
2 tbsp freshly-squeezed lemon juice
salt and freshly ground pepper

Cut off the tender tips of the purslane sprigs. Chop the cucumber, tomatoes and spring onion. Finely dice the feta cheese.

Mix together the purslane, cucumber, tomatoes and spring onion. Toss with olive oil and lemon juice. Season with salt and freshly ground pepper. Sprinkle over feta cubes and serve.

Purslane Salad

PEACH FILO PARCELS

F ilo pastry, paper-fine sheets of pastry, is usually sold frozen but sometimes found chilled. Filo is wonderfully versatile and in Greek cooking crops up in a number of both savoury and sweet dishes from spinach-stuffed spanakopitakia to syrup-laden baklava. As you buy it in sheets (ready-rolled so to speak) it's quick and simple to use. The only thing to remember is that it dries out and becomes brittle very quickly so should be kept covered with a damp clean tea-towel or sheet of cling film.

Here filo is used to make an elegant summer-time dessert.

Ingredients (serves four)

55 g/2 oz unsalted butter
4 ripe peaches
8 sheets of filo pastry (30 cm/12 in x 18 cm/7 in)
4 tsp semolina
225 g/8 oz raspberries
1 tbsp icing sugar

Melt the butter. Pour boling water over the peaches, scald them briefly then drain. Peel and slice in half, removing central stone.
Preheat oven to Gas Mark 5/375F/190C.
Take one sheet of filo pastry and brush with melted butter. Top with another sheet of filo and brush with melted butter. Sprinkle one teaspoon of semolina in the centre of the filo. Place the two peach halves on top of each other over the semolina. Gather up the filo pastry around the peach and twist the top of the pastry together to form a money-pouch shape. Repeat process to make four filo parcels in all. Place filo parcels on a baking tray and brush them with melted butter. Bake in the oven for 20 minutes, until golden-brown.
While peach parcels are baking blend together the raspberries and icing sugar to make a smooth puree. Strain puree through a fine-meshed sieve.
Serve the peach parcels warm from the oven with the raspberry puree.

STELLA'S SEMOLINA CAKE

S tella Christofi (Maria Yiannoullou's daughter) has a passionate interest in food, cooking traditional Cypriot dishes, such as this cake, but also experimenting with other cuisines, for instance, Chinese or North African. This cake uses semolina and crushed almonds rather than flour which gives it a particular flavour and texture. Stella crushes the almonds by putting them in a clean tea-towel and banging them with a rolling pin as the uneven-sized pieces give the cake a more interesting texture. It can also be baked in a rectangular tin (25.5 cm/10 in x 27 cm/12 in) and cut into small squares with an almond arranged in each square. In this version the syrup is flavoured with rosewater. Alternately Stella suggests making a simple sugar syrup (without the spices) and flavouring it with Grand Marnier.

Ingredients (makes one 23 cm/9 in cake)

225 g/8 oz (+ 1 tsp) unsalted butter
115 g/4 oz almonds (skins left on)
5 eggs
175 g/6 oz sugar
2 tbsp brandy
1 tsp grated lemon rind
350 g/12 oz semolina
2 tsp baking powder
½ tsp ground cloves
pinch of salt
a few blanched almonds for decoration

Syrup

850 ml/1½ pts water
8 oz/225 g sugar
4 cloves
1 cinnamon stick
2-3 tbsp rosewater

Preheat oven to Gas Mark 4/180C/350F. Grease a 23 cm/9 in cake tin with the teaspoon of butter.

Separate the eggs. Finely crush the almonds. Cream butter until soft. Beat in sugar and gradually mix in the egg yolks, making sure they are well incorporated. Mix in brandy and lemon rind.

Gradually add in the semolina, baking powder, ground cloves, chopped almonds and salt, stirring until well blended.

In a separate bowl beat the egg white until they form soft peaks. Fold beaten egg white into semolina mixture.

Pour semolina mixture into buttered cake tin. Top with blanched almonds. Bake for 1 hour. Test that the cake is cooked through by poking a skewer into the centre of the cake. If the skewer is clean when withdrawn then the cake is cooked through.

While the cake is cooking make the sugar syrup. Dissolve sugar in water over a low heat. Add in cloves and cinnamon stick. Simmer for 5-10 minutes until desired consistency is reached. Remove from heat and stir in rose water.

Allow the syrup to cool slightly. Pierce the top of the baked cake with a skewer and slowly pour over sugar syrup until absorbed.

GREEK CYPRIOT

RECOMMENDED COOKBOOKS

A Book of Mediterranean Food,
Elizabeth David.
A knowledgeable and evocative book, written by Elizabeth David during the grey austerity of post-war Britain to re-capture the Mediterranean flavours she hungered for.

The Cooking of Greece and Turkey,
Rena Salaman.
An appetizingly illustrated cookbook published by Sainsbury's.

Mediterranean Cookery,
Claudia Roden.
A well-written and attractive book, dealing with the Mediterranean as a whole, filled with tempting recipes.

GREEK GLOSSARY

Bulgar (pourgouri): parboiled, cracked wheat grains, available either coarse or finely ground.

Cheeses: anari, a soft cheese, similar to Italian ricotta; feta, a salty, crumbly white cheese made from cow's, sheep's or goat's milk, often stored in brine to retain its freshness; halloumi, a firm white cheese with a rubbery texture, often flavoured with mint.

Colocassi: a large, brown, fibrous tuber with a distinctive white stump, which is a staple of Cypriot cookery.

Filo: paper-thin pastry, sometimes spelled 'phyllo', used in both sweet and savoury dishes. It's usually available frozen, but occasionally fresh filo can be found. When using filo be careful not too let it dry out and become brittle.

Glyko: preserved fresh fruit, such as quinces and cherries, in a sweet syrup, traditionally offered to guests with coffee.

Kataifi: a vermicelli-like pastry, formed by pouring batter through a fine sieve on to a hot surface, usually found frozen.

Loundza: smoked pork loin, a traditional Cypriot Christmas food.

Louvana: a type of vetch, recognisable by its curly tendrils, eaten as a salad leaf.

Mahlepi: the fragrant kernel of the blackcherry stone, sold in husked form and added to sweet yeast breads.

Mastic: the fragrant resin of an evergreen tree, sold in powdered form for use in sweet yeast breads.

Olive oil: in Greek mythology the olive tree was a gift to the Greeks from Athena. The rich, fruity oil extracted from olives is the cooking fat of Greece, adding a distinctive flavour.

Olives: Kalamata, named after the city, are the famous, large, black-purple olives. Tiasis, or cracked olives, are partially crushed olives which have been marinated, often with olive oil, lemon slices, garlic and cumin seeds.

Ouzo: clear, anise-flavoured liquor, distilled from grapes. When diluted this potent aperitif becomes white and cloudy and is nicknamed 'lion's milk'.

Parsley: the flat-leafed, flavourful variety known as 'continental parsley' is a basic herb in Greek cookery.

Pasta: dried pasta is a legacy of the Italian influence on Greek cookery. Shapes include macarona, long thick tubes of pasta, manestra, pasta kernels and vermicelli, often cooked with bulgar.

Purslane (glysterida): a green salad vegetable with rounded clover-shaped leaves, it is sometimes called 'Cypriot watercress'.

Retsina: wine with a distinctive resin flavour, traced back to the days when wine was kept in goat skins sealed with pitch.

Rocket (rocca): a green salad leaf with a distinctive peppery flavour, now very fashionable.

Sausages: bastourma, dark, short, spiced sausages; loukanika, thin sausages popularly flavoured with allspice, savory and orange peel or coriander seeds.

Savory: a peppery-flavoured herb, which looks similar to thyme.

Tahini: a smooth paste made from pounded sesame seeds.

Tarama: smoked grey mullet roe or, more commonly, cod roe, used to make taramasalata.

Trahani: brown, stubby, crumbly tubes made from fermented cracked wheat and yogurt. They have a tangy flavour and should be soaked before using.

Vine leaves: large, distinctively shaped leaves, used principally to make dolmades. Occasionally found fresh but usually preserved in brine, when they need soaking to rinse off excess salt.

Yogurt: thick, creamy Greek yogurt, made from either sheep's or cow's milk.

GREEK CYPRIOT

A TRIP TO AN ITALIAN DELI: NINE RECIPES

POLENTA CROSTINI CON FEGATINI
BALSAMIC GAZPACHO
BUFFALO MOZZARELLA, COURGETTE & ROCKET SALAD
ANNABELLE'S ANGEL'S HAIR WITH PORCINI
SEAFOOD RISOTTO
SALSICCE AL POMODORO
ARTURO'S POLENTA CON FRITTO
AMARETTI APRICOT CRUMBLE
PANETTONE PUDDING

Ten years ago if I wanted to buy even everyday Italian ingredients such as ricotta cheese or risotto rice I had to visit an Italian delicatessen. Now Italian cooking is both fashionable and popular with Italian ingredients widely available. The traditional Italian delis, which started life as a down-to-earth foodshop serving the Italian community, now face competition both from supermarkets and from fashionable new-wave foodshops, stocked to the gills with Mediterranean ingredients such as olive oil, sun-dried tomatoes and balsamic vinegar.

Thankfully the best of the Italian delis, such as Soho veterans I Camisa on Old Compton Street (0171 437 7610) and Lina Stores on Brewer Street (0171 437 6482), still survive. They continue to offer an unbeatable combination of sociable, helpful staff and a high quality of ingredients, whether homemade fresh pasta, chunks of Parmesan or marinated olives, which the supermarkets can't match.

I Camisa

POLENTA CROSTINI CON FEGATINI

Polenta, ground cornmeal, is one of Italy's great comfort foods. Instant polenta (which I've used here) is extremely quick and easy to use while unprocessed polenta requires rather more loving attention as it takes around 40 minutes of constant stirring.

Polenta can be eaten in two forms: either as a liquid 'porridge' (as in Arturo's recipe on p.68) or allowed to set and then cut into squares. Here grilled polenta squares have been topped with a classic Tuscan crostini topping made from chicken livers.

Ingredients (serves four as a first course)

115g/4oz instant polenta
600ml/1 pt cold water
salt

Fegatini

1 clove garlic
225g/8oz chicken livers
3 tbsp extra virgin olive oil
1 tbsp marsala/medium sherry
pinch of grated nutmeg
salt and freshly ground pepper
15g/½oz fresh basil

Place polenta and water in a large saucepan. Season with salt. Bring to the boil and stir well. Reduce heat, cover and simmer gently until thickened. Pour polenta into a greased baking tin (18cm/7in x 25.5cm/10cm) and leave for an hour to set.

While polenta is setting make the fegatini topping. Peel and chop garlic.

Heat 2 tbsp olive oil in frying pan. Fry the garlic until softened. Add the chicken livers and fry until browned but still pink and juicy inside. Add in marsala or sherry, nutmeg, salt and freshly ground pepper and cook briefly. Blend chicken livers into a paste.

Cut the set polenta into 16 squares. Brush with 1 tbsp olive oil and grill until browned. Set aside to cool.

Spread fegatini topping on to the grilled polenta squares. Shred basil and sprinkle over the fegatini crostini.

BALSAMIC GAZPACHO

During the eighties in Britain balsamic vinegar suddenly became the fashionable condiment and is now widely available. Balsamic vinegar ranges enormously in price, from the affordable sharper mass-produced young vinegar to the lovingly nurtured vintage vinegar several decades old. Its rich sweet flavour lends itself to salad dressings and meat dishes while a few drops sprinkled on to strawberries enhances their flavour. Here it's used to zip up a classic Spanish chilled summer soup. For best results use the ripest and most flavourful tomatoes you can find.

Ingredients (serves four)

1½ lb/700 g ripe tomatoes
1 small cucumber
1 red pepper
1 onion
1 clove garlic
4 tbsp olive oil
4 tbsp balsamic vinegar
450 ml/¾ pt water
150 ml/¼ pt tomato juice
salt

Garnish

finely diced cucumber
finely diced green pepper
finely diced tomato
garlic bread croutons

Chop tomatoes and cucumber. De-seed and chop red pepper. Peel and chop onion and garlic.

Process together tomatoes, cucumber, red pepper, onion, garlic, olive oil, balsamic vinegar, water and tomato juice. Strain, pressing down on the mixture to squeeze out liquid. Season to taste with salt. Cover and chill until serving.

Serve with the garnish ingredients above.

BUFFALO MOZZARELLA, COURGETTE & ROCKET SALAD

Buffalo mozzarella, as opposed to cow's milk mozzarella, has a delicious rich tanginess which justifies its higher price tag. Here it's combined with marinated fried courgettes and fresh rocket leaves to make a rich salad. Serve with focaccia or ciabatta for a first course.

Ingredients (serves four as a first course)

450 g/1 lb courgettes
salt and freshly ground pepper
oil for shallow-frying
1 clove garlic
1 tbsp olive oil
grated zest of 1 lemon
1 tsp balsamic vinegar
1 tbsp pine nuts
150 g/5½ oz buffalo mozzarella
1 bunch rocket

Slice the courgettes finely lengthwise into long narrow slices. Sprinkle with salt and set aside for 20 minutes to draw out any bitter juices. Rinse well, drain and pat dry.

Heat oil for shallow-frying in a large frying pan. Fry the courgette slices until browned on both sides. Remove with a slotted spoon and drain on kitchen paper. Peel and chop garlic. Mix together fried courgette slices, garlic, olive oil, lemon zest and balsamic vinegar. Season with freshly ground pepper. Cover and set aside to marinate for at 2 hours.

Dry-fry the pine nuts until golden. Slice the buffalo mozzarella. Shred the rocket.

Assemble the salad by placing the rocket in a serving dish. Top with marinated courgette slices then sliced mozzarella. Sprinkle over dry-fried pine nuts. Season with salt and pepper and serve.

ANNABELLE'S ANGEL'S HAIR WITH PORCINI

A stay in Italy as a teenage au-pair came as a culinary revelation to Annabelle Pangborn. She was impressed at how even the simplest foods were so flavourful and also at just how versatile pasta was.

On coming to living in London Annabelle hunted out Italian delis, buying her coffee from the Algerian Coffee Stores and fresh pasta from Lina Stores or I Camisa.

Porcini (Italian dried ceps) add a distinctive richness to this recipe, combined with fine stands of capelli d'angelo or angel's hair pasta to make a simple but intensely flavourful dish. The finishing touch is the freshly grated pecorino romano, a sheep's milk cheese.

Ingredients (serves two)

25 g/1 oz porcini
225 g/8 oz mixture of field and organic
mushrooms (button mushrooms "just won't
do!" according to Annabelle)
2 cloves garlic
a few sprigs of flat-leaf parsley
salt and freshly ground pepper
4 tbsp olive oil
a few sprigs of thyme
225 g-280 g/8-10 oz dried angel's hair pasta
55 g/2 oz freshly grated Pecorino romano, to
serve

Cover the porcini with warm water and soak for 20 minutes. Drain porcini and reserve soaking water, straining it to remove any grit. Pat the porcini dry and roughly chop.

Slice the field and organic mushrooms. Peel and chop garlic. Roughly chop the parsley.

Set a large pan of salted water for the pasta to boil. Heat the olive oil in a large, heavy-bottomed frying pan. Add the garlic and gently fry until golden. Remove the garlic and discard. Add the sliced fresh mushrooms to the pan and fry over a high heat for a few minutes. Reduce the heat, season well with salt and freshly ground pepper. Add in the porcini and thyme sprigs and cook gently.

At this point add the angel's hair pasta to the boiling water. Cook until al dente. Drain and add to the mushrooms. Add in reserved porcini water and chopped parsley. Toss well, cover and leave to stand for 4-5 minutes to allow the flavours to infuse. Remove the thyme stalks and serve with freshly grated pecorino.

SEAFOOD RISOTTO

Risotto is one of my favourite dishes, another great Italian comfort food. Arborio rice is ideal for risottos as it can soak up large amounts of liquid without becoming soggy.

Risotto is a very versatile dish which can be made with any number of ingredients, from vegetables such as spinach or pumpkin to chicken livers or Italian sausage. This is a luxurious seafood version, garnished with tiger prawns and scallops. Homemade fish stock is quick and simple to make with fish bone trimmings from a fishmonger. If you are making your own fish stock add in the raw prawn heads for extra flavour.

Ingredients (serves four)

1 onion
2 cloves garlic
1 red pepper
8 raw tiger prawns
450g/1lb cleaned squid
1.2 ltr/2 pt fish stock
8 tbsp olive oil
4 tbsp chopped flat-leaf parsley
350g/12oz arborio rice
salt and freshly ground pepper
4 cleaned, trimmed scallops

Peel and chop onion and garlic. De-seed and finely chop red pepper. Peel tiger prawns, removing heads if on, and de-veining. Roughly chop four of the prawns, keeping the remaining prawns intact. Chop the squid into small pieces.

Bring the fish stock to a gently rolling boil in a large saucepan. Heat 6 tbsp olive oil in a large, heavy-bottomed saucepan. Fry the onions until translucent then add in the garlic. Fry briefly and add in red pepper, squid, chopped prawns and 2 tbsp chopped parsley. Cook, stirring, for 2-3 minutes.

Mix in the rice, stirring well. Season with salt and freshly ground pepper.

Add in the hot fish stock a ladle at a time, stirring constantly. As the stock is absorbed by the rice add in another ladleful of stock. After around 15 minutes the rice should be tender. Cover and keep warm.

Heat the remaining 2 tbsp olive oil in a small frying pan. Fry the prawns and scallops until just cooked, a matter of minutes.

Divide the seafood risotto among four warmed serving plates. Top each plateful with a fried prawn and scallop. Sprinkle over remaining parsley and serve at once.

SALSICCE AL POMODORO

S trings of Italian sausages or salsicce can be found in good Italian delis. While visibly fatty they are also much tastier than the bland mass-produced bangers found in British supermarkets.

This is a robust dish which should be served with polenta, pasta or mashed potato to soak up the tasty sauce.

Ingredients (serves four)

1 red pepper
1 red onion
1 clove garlic
450 g/1 lb spicy Italian sausages (salsicce)
1 tbsp olive oil
1 bay leaf
400 g tin chopped tomatoes
1 tsp fennel seeds
salt and freshly ground pepper
8 basil leaves

Salsicce

Grill red pepper until charred all over. Wrap in a plastic bag and set aside to cool (this makes the pepper easier to peel). Once cool enough to handle, peel, de-seed and slice into short strips.

Peel and chop onion and garlic. Chop sausages into large chunks.

Heat olive oil in a large frying pan. Fry onion, garlic and bay leaf until fragrant. Add sausage chunks and fry until they lose their raw look. Add in chopped tomatoes, fennel seeds, red pepper strips, salt and freshly ground pepper. Tear basil and add in.

Cook over medium heat until sausages are cooked through and the sauce is thickened.

ARTURO'S POLENTA CON FRITTO

Arturo Tosi learned to cook "for survival, when I came to this country". A true Italian in his love of good flavourful food he despises supermarkets preferring instead to shop at small local shops, among them the excellent and ever-busy Golborne Fisheries on Golborne Road.

This dish is in Arturo's own words "an unusual combination which has Venetian elements and a little touch of Chinese." The polenta (cornmeal) of the title is cooked to a fairly liquid consistency ("no thicker than humous") and topped with a 'fritto', a mixture of fried fish and prawns. Ingeniously Arturo combines "incredibly cheap" small "7 cm long" jacks or sprats (which he fillets himself) with rather more expensive tiger prawns. The proportion of luxurious prawns to cheap jacks can vary according to how much money you wish to spend. To make it succesfully Arturo warns that "you need to cook it very carefully, very fast and at the last minute."

Ingredients (serves six)

12 raw tiger prawns
salt and freshly ground pepper
a little flour
30 small jacks or sprats
450 g/1 lb Kenyan green beans
300 ml/½ pt chicken stock
7 garlic clove
1 spring onion
2 lemons
2 ltr/3½ pt water
2 tbsp corn oil
pinch of sugar
½ tbsp sherry
dash of soy sauce
1 oz/25 g butter
375 g pkt instant polenta

Peel, de-head, de-vein and wash tiger prawns. Season with salt and pepper, toss in a little flour and set aside.Cut the heads off the sprats and fillet them. Wash them, pat dry, season with salt and pepper and set aside.

Top and tail the green beans. Place the chicken stock in a saucepan. Bring to the boil, add in green beans. Cover and cook for around 15 minutes by which time the beans should have absorbed most of the stock. Set aside. Peel the garlic cloves, finely chopping one but leaving the others whole. Trim and finely chop spring onion. Slice lemons into wedges.

In a large saucepan bring 2 ltrs/3½ pts of salted water to the boil for the polenta.

Meanwhile heat 1 tbsp corn oil in a large frying pan. Gently fry the chopped garlic and spring onion until softened. Add in the green beans and increase the heat. Add in a little pinch of sugar, salt, freshly grated pepper, ½ tbsp sherry and a dash of soy sauce. Mix well, cook briefly, cover and keep warm.

Heat a further 1 tbsp corn oil in a large frying pan. Quickly fry the jack fillets until cooked, turning them over in the process. Be very careful not to overcook them. Set aside to keep warm.

Melt the butter in a frying pan. Add garlic cloves. When fragrant add in prawns. Fry prawns very gently until they turn pink, again being careful not to overcook them.

Add in polenta to the pan of boiling water, stirring vigorously and constantly to prevent any lumps from forming. Stirring bring to the boil when it will thicken and begin to bubble. Reduce heat and simmer gently for a few minutes stirring.

Divide the polenta among six dishes. Top each plateful with fried jacks, prawns and green beans. Serve with lemon wedges.

AMARETTI APRICOT CRUMBLE

Apricots and almonds are a blissful combination. Crushed amaretti (almond macaroons) and ground almonds make a rich, sweet crumbly topping for this simple dessert. Vanilla sugar is much used in Italian baking and can either be bought or made at home by simply placing a couple of vanilla pods in a jar of caster sugar and leaving them to infuse.

Serve the crumble warm from the oven with whipped cream or vanilla ice-cream.

Ingredients

450g/1lb apricots
8 amaretti biscuits
55g/2oz plain flour
115g/4oz ground almonds
115g/4oz butter
55g/2oz vanilla sugar

Scald the apricots with boiling water. Leave to stand for a few minutes, drain, peel and halve, discarding stones. Roughly crush amaretti biscuits. Mix flour and ground almonds in a mixing bowl. Cube butter and rub in with fingertips until absorbed. Mix in vanilla sugar and crushed amaretti.

Place apricot halves in a heatproof serving dish. Top with amaretti mixture. Bake for 30 minutes at Gas Mark 5/375F/190C until golden-brown.

Panettone

PANETTONE PUDDING

I n Italy panettone, a large light yeast cake flavoured with sultanas and citrus peel, is a traditional Christmas treat. Italian delicatessens, both here and in Italy, hang the pre-packed panettone in clusters from the ceiling like lanterns. Panettone is delicious either eaten cold or lightly toasted. Here it's used in a rich version of bread and butter pudding, delicious served with a fresh raspberry puree (see p.55 for recipe).

Ingredients (serves four to six)

25 g/1 oz butter
350 g/ ¾ lb panettone
300 ml/½ pt milk
284 ml double cream
2 eggs
75 g/3 oz vanilla sugar
25 g/1 oz sultanas

Melt butter. Slice panettone into large cubes.

Heat together milk and cream, bringing to boiling point. Meanwhile, beat together eggs and vanilla sugar in a large mixing bowl. Pour in scalding creamy milk, mixing well.

Preheat oven to Gas Mark 3/325F/170C. Layer panettone cubes and sultanas in a buttered ovenproof dish. Pour over melted butter, then egg mixture.

Place dish in a deep baking tray. Pour hot water in around the dish so that the water comes halfway up around it. Bake for 50 minutes to 1 hour.

ITALIAN

RECOMMENDED COOKBOOKS

Antonio Carluccio's Italian Feast
Written with zest by funghi-phile and restaurateur Antonio Carluccio, this is an appetising exploration of northern Italy.

Classic Food of Northern Italy, Gastronomy of Italy and Secrets of an Italian Kitchen
Anna del Conte.
Three wonderful books on La Cucina Italiana by an authoritative and readable writer. The first and the third titles are imaginative cookbooks while the second is a useful encyclopedia of Italian food.

The Classic Italian Cookbook, The Second Classic Italian Cookbook and Marcella's Kitchen
Marcella Hazan.
Essential cookbooks for anyone interested in Italian food by the doyenne of Italian cookery.

The Food of Italy
Claudia Roden.
A beautifully-written guide to the regions of Italy and their distinctive dishes, both evocative and usable.

Italian Food
Elizabeth David.
Although published in 1954, her comments on the essence of Italian cookery remain perceptive and valid. A classic.

ITALIAN GLOSSARY

Balsamic vinegar: an aromatic brown vinegar made from wine must and historically from Modena. Traditionally matured balsamic vinegar is very expensive, while cheaper, commercially produced balsamic vinegar compresses the maturing process into a few years.

Ciabatta: a flavourful, distinctively textured bread, named after a house-shoe because of its flattened, oval shape

Foccacia: a flat, salty bread flavoured with olive oil and sometimes additionally with rosemary, onions or sage, known as schiacciata in Tuscany.

Fontina: a semi-soft cow's milk cheese, traditionally from Val d'Aosta, and famously used to make fonduta, a fondue flavoured with white truffles.

Marscapone: an extremely rich cream cheese, an essential ingredient for the popular dessert tiramisu.

Mozzarella: a bland white cheese with a rubbery texture that is famously used on pizzas. Buffalo's milk mozzarella is more expensive than the more easily found cow's milk version. Baby mozzarellas are called 'bocconcini'

Olive oil: a key ingredient in Italian cooking, olive oil is labelled according to its acidity levels. Extra Virgin must have no more than 1% acidity. As with wine, different regions produce different-flavoured olive oils, with Tuscan olive oil being famously piquant.

Panettone: a light, brioche-style cake, containing sultanas, traditionally given at Christmas time, which is when the Italian delis stock several varieties.

Parmesan: the best-known Italian cheese and also the largest and longest-matured cheese produced in Italy, this hard-grating cheese comes traditionally from around Parma. Grana padano is a similar cheese produced in Lombardy. Buy chunks of Parmesan and keep them refrigerated, wrapped in foil, to be used as required.

Pasta: this famous Italian staple comes both fresh and dried and in a multiplicity of forms. Fresh pasta, made with eggs, can be bought ready-made from delicatessens. Dried pasta should be made from durum wheat and popular Italian brands include Barilla and Da Cecco.

Pecorino: a hard sheep's milk cheese. Pecorino Romano is most commonly found but there is also Pecorino Sardo, from Sardinia, and Toscana, from Tuscany.

Pine nuts: small ivory-coloured kernels from the stone pine tree, with a distinctive flavour.

Polenta: a Northern Italian staple made from maize, polenta flour is available in fine or coarse versions. Precooked polenta flour, scorned by purists, is also available.

Porcini: wild Boletus mushrooms, prized for their flavour and priced accordingly. Dried porcini mushrooms, often in pieces, are easily found, while fresh porcini are much rarer.

Prosciutto Crudo: the most famous of these salt-cured hams is Parma ham, cured for 14 months. San Daniele, cured for 12 months, is considered another fine prosciutto.

Ricotta: A light, bland sheep's whey cheese, drained in baskets which give it its distinctive woven markings. It is used in both sweet and savoury dishes.

Rocket: known as 'rucola', this peppery, jagged leaf is increasingly available as a chic salad leaf. Italians are fond of pointing out that in Italy it grows wild as a weed.

Salami: ready-to-eat salt-cured sausages, available in a range of sizes and flavours, such as fine-textured Milano or finocchiona, flavoured with fennel.

Salsiccie: Italian sausages, usually made from pork. Luganega is a mild sausage from Lombardy, sold in long narrow coils, while in the South chilli is often added as a flavouring

Sun-dried tomatoes: as their name suggests, these are dried tomatoes, available either in their dry state or preserved in olive oil.

A TRIP TO A JAPANESE SUPERMARKET: FIVE RECIPES

VEGETERIAN TEMPURA MEDLEY
SOBA NOODLES IN SOUP
SESAME CHICKEN CROQUETTES
MISO AUBERGINE SALAD
WASABI SALMON

Once Japanese restaurants in London were the sedate preserve of a wealthy business elite. Now with sushi on sale in sandwich bars and the proliferation of Wagamama-style noodle bars, Japanese food has become far more accessible and popular.

For those who want to cook Japanese food at home there are a number of Japanese foodstores dotted around London, mainly in North and West London serving local Japanese communities. Of these the largest and most comprehensive is Yaohan Supermarket, at Yaohan Plaza in Colindale (399 Edgware Road, NW9, 0181-450 0422). Gleamingly spic and span, with ingredients helpfully labelled in both English and Japanese, Yaohan has an impressive stock of fresh fish, meat, fresh produce and store-cupboard staples. Furthermore, the supermarket is handily positioned next to the Plaza's Food Court where whetted appetites can be satisfied with an assortment of Japanese goodies, including excellent sushi and a variety of noodle dishes.

Yaohan Plaza

VEGETERIAN TEMPURA MEDLEY

This version of a classic deep-fried Japanese dish called tempura is a delicious combination of elements: sweet, dense, orange-fleshed kabocha pumpkin, crisp green beans, delicate oyster mushrooms and crisp curls of nori seaweed, all coated in a light, airy batter.

Ingredients (serves four)

85 g/3 oz green beans
85 g/3 oz oyster mushrooms
350 g/12 oz kobocha pumpkin
a 21 cm/8 ¼in x 19 cm/7¼ in sheet of nori
1 egg
225 ml/8 fl oz ice-cold water
140 g/5 oz plain flour
oil for deep frying

Dipping sauce

1 cm/½ in root ginger
50 ml/2 fl oz Japanese soy sauce

Oyster Mushrooms

Top and tail green beans and slice each bean across into two pieces. Separate oyster mushrooms into single mushrooms if in a cluster. Cut skin off kabocha pumpkin and slice finely. Cut nori into 16-20 small squares.

Prepare the dipping sauce by peeling and finely grating the root ginger and mixing it into the soy sauce.

Break the egg into a mixing bowl. Using a pair of chopsticks beat in the water. Tip in the flour and mix briefly to form a lumpy batter. Be very careful not to overmix.

Heat the oil in a large, deep pan. Dip oyster mushrooms and kabocha pumpkin slices into batter. Coat the nori squares on one side only. Make small bundles of the green beans and coat these.

Fry the battered ingredients in the hot oil for around two minutes until pale gold, turning over once in the process. Remove with a slotted spoon and drain on a paper towel. Serve at once with the ginger dipping sauce.

SOBA NOODLES IN SOUP

J apanese noodles range from broad wheat noodles called udon to thread-like, transparent cellophane noodles made from mung beans. This hearty soup recipe uses slender brown soba noodles (made from buckwheat) which have delicious, slightly nutty flavour. The soup is made quickly and simply using the Japanese equivalent of stock cubes, a packet of bonito flavoured soup stock or dashi-no-moto.

Ingredients (serves four)

150 g/5½oz pork fillet
30 ml/1 fl oz (+ 1 tbsp) mirin (Japanese rice wine)
30 ml/1 fl oz (+ 1 tbsp) Japanese soy sauce
10 g pkt of dashi no-moto-stock
250 g pkt of soba noodles
450 g/1 lb fresh spinach
2 spring onions

Slice pork fillet into fine strips. Toss with 1 tbsp mirin and 1 tbsp soy sauce. Cover and marinate in the fridge for 1 hour.

Make up dashi stock by adding 1 ltr/1¾ pt of boiling water to the dashi-no-moto stock. Bring stock to a rolling boil in a large saucepan. Add marinated pork strips and simmer for 15 minutes. Remove any skum on the soup. Mix in 30 ml/1 fl oz mirin and 30 ml/1 fl oz Japanese soy sauce.

Meanwhile rinse spinach thoroughly and cook in a large pan of boiling water until just cooked; drain, squeeze dry, shape into a 'roll' and slice across into 8 slices. Trim and finely chop spring onions. Bring large pan of boiling water to the boil. Add in soba noodles. Bring the water to the boil and pour in 225 ml/8 fl oz cold water. Bring the water to the boil once more. Add in a further 225 ml/8 fl oz cold water and bring to the boil. Drain the noodles and rinse under a hot tap.

Divide the soba noodles among four serving bowls. Pour over soup, dividing pork slices among the four bowls. Divide spinach roll slices and chopped spring onion among bowls and serve at once.

JAPANESE

SESAME CHICKEN CROQUETTES

Traditionally meat is consumed in smaller quanitities in Japanese cuisine and the meat counter at a Japanese supermarket is consequently a daintier affair than a British meat counter. Instead of great joints of meat one finds bamboo leaf chicken breasts (the small fillets found attached to a chicken breast fillet) and wafer-thin slices of beef for shabu shabu. This recipe uses minced chicken, sold in Japanese supermarkets or easily made at home if you have a food processor.

Serve with rice and stir-fried green beans for a quick, tasty meal.

Ingredients (serves four)

2.5 cm/1 in root ginger
1 spring onion
400 g/14 oz minced chicken
2 tbsp sesame seeds
1 tsp sesame oil
1 tbsp Japanese soy sauce
1 tbsp groundnut oil

Peel and finely grate ginger. Trim and finely chop spring onion, both white and green parts.

Mix together minced chicken, ginger, spring onion, sesame seeds, sesame oil and soy sauce. Shape into eight small croquettes.

Heat groundnut oil in a large frying pan. Fry croquettes until golden-brown on both sides and cooked through.

Soy Sauce

MISO AUBERGINE SALAD

E ven the smallest Japanese foodstore is sure to stock at least a few packets of vacuum-packed miso paste, while Yaohan has several shelvfulls. Made from fermented cooked soy beans this is an essential Japanese flavouring, adding a rich salty-sweetness to soups, marinades and sauces. Miso ranges in colour and flavour. White miso is lighter and more delicate in flavour than red miso, which is fermented for longer and consequently has a stronger, more robust taste.

This recipe is for a rich and very flavourful aubergine salad which goes well with rice.

Ingredients (serves two as a main dish or four as a side-dish)

1 large aubergine
salt
1 tbsp sesame seeds
3 tbsp red or brown miso
1 tbsp Japanese soy sauce
1 tbsp mirin
1 tbsp sugar
1 spring onion
3 tbsp groundnut oil
3 tbsp chopped flat-leaf parsley

Miso

Cut aubergine into small dice about 1 cm/½ in square. Sprinkle over salt and set aside for half an hour to draw out bitter juices. Rinse and pat dry.

Gently dry-fry sesame seeds, stirring often, until golden-brown. Mix together miso, soy sauce, mirin and sugar into smooth paste. Trim and finely chop spring onion, both white and green parts.

Heat wok. Add oil. Stir-fry diced aubergine until golden-brown. Transfer to serving dish. Mix with miso paste, spring onion and parsley. Sprinkle over sesame seeds and serve while warm.

WASABI SALMON

S ushi fans will be familiar with wasabi, the bright-green Japanese horseradish paste often used to flavour sushi. Wasabi is sold in powdered form (which needs mixing with water) or ready-prepared in small toothpaste-like tubes.
Here the tanginess of the wasabi coating cuts through the richness of the salmon. Serve with rice and a vegetable side-dish.

Ingredients

2 spring onions
8 tsp wasabi paste
grated zest of 2 limes
1½ tbsp oil
2 tbsp fine breadcrumbs
1 egg
4 x 140 g/5 oz pieces of salmon fillet
4 tsp of sushi gari (pickled ginger)

Preheat grill. Trim and finely chop spring onions, both white and green parts. Mix together wasabi, spring onion, lime zest, oil and breadcrumbs.

Beat egg. Dip salmon fillet pieces in egg then in wasabi mixture, coating all sides.

Grill salmon until cooked through, turning pieces over once. Serve with pickled ginger.

RECOMMENDED COOKBOOKS

The Heart of Zen Cookery,
Soei Yoneda.
An elegant tome, exploring the centuries-old Zen temple vegetarian cuisine.

Japanese Cookery,
Elizabeth Lambert Ortiz.
Clearly written, this is a useful introduction to the complexities of the cuisine.

Step-by-Step Japanese Cooking,
Leslie Downer and Minoru Yoneda.
A clear and accessible book, designed as an introduction to Japanese cuisine.

Way of the Noodle,
Russell Cronin.
An entertaining insight into Wagamama, the cult noodle bar.

JAPANESE GLOSSARY

Agar agar (kanten): a vegetarian setting agent obtained from seaweed, available either in powdered form or in translucent strands.

Azuki beans: small dark red beans. In a sweetened paste form (an), they form a principal ingredient in Japanese cakes.

Bean curd (tofu): an ivory-coloured soy bean product with a firm custard texture, available either fresh or vacuum-packed. Kinu or silk tofu has a more delicate texture than momen or cotton tofu. Koyadofu is freeze-dried tofu, dull brown with a spongy texture. Aburage are thin deep-fried sheets of bean curd.

Bonito: dried bonito flakes, together with kombu seaweed, are used to make dashi soup stock and also as a garnish. Dashi-no-moto is an instant granule form of dashi stock, available in packets.

Burdock (gobo): A long slender root vegetable, available fresh and canned.

Chrysanthemum leaves (shungiku): the leaves of the edible garland chrysanthemum (not to be confused with our ornamental inedible one), used as a garnish and a vegetable.

Daikon: a large, long, mild, white radish, also called mooli in greengrocers. Dried daikon strips, called kiriboshi daikon, need soaking before use.

81

Fish and seafood: raw fish, either in sashimi or sushi, is one of the most famous elements of Japanese cuisine. Popular fish include mackerel (saba), salmon (sake) and tuna (maguro), with the latter graded according to its fattiness. Grilled eel (unagi) is a prized delicacy. Popular seafood includes abalone (awabi), horse clams (mirugai), scallops (hotategai), salmon roe (ikura), octopus (tako) and squid (ika).

Fishcakes and fish sausages: boiled, baked and deep-fried fishcakes and sausages come in various forms, and are often found in the deep-freeze section. Popular varieties include: naruto maki: a fish sausage with a spiral pink or yellow pattern running through it; satsuma-age: oval-shaped fried fishcake; chukuwu: a fish sausage with a hole running through it.

Flours: rice flour (joshinko) is used for savoury doughs. Glutinous rice flour (mochiko) and soya bean flour (kinako) are used mainly for desserts.

Gingko nuts (ginnan): maidenhair tree kernels. Fresh gingko nuts, which need shelling, are ivory-cloured, while tinned, shelled gingko nuts are pale green.

Kabocha: Japanese pumpkin, often sold deep-frozen.

Kampyo: dried gourd or winter melon strips, used for tying food.

Kinome: prickly ash tree leaf, used as a garnish.

Konnyaku: a bland, glutinous substance made from the root of the devil's tongue plant, often labelled 'alimentary paste' and found in the chilled section or freezer. Konnyaku noodles, called shirataki (meaning white waterfall), are sold packaged in water.

Kuzu: a white starch made from the kuzu vine root, sometimes labelled 'kuzu arrowroot'.

Lotus root (renkon): a crunchy root with a decorative tracery of holes, available fresh, in sausage-like links, or tinned.

Mirin: a sweet Japanese rice wine, used as a glazing ingredient.

Miso: fermented soya bean paste, available in a variety of colours and flavours. It is usually found in the chilled or freezer section and should be stored in the fridge.

Mochi: cooked glutinous rice, pounded to a paste.

Mountain yam (yama no imo): a large, pale-skinned sweet-flavoured tuber, which comes in different shapes.

Mushrooms: these include large, brown-capped shitake (available both fresh and dried), tiny white-capped clusters of enokidake, light brown shimeji and large, brown matsutake.

Natto: fermented soya beans with a pungent smell and sticky texture. Packets of it can be found in deep-freeze sections.

Noodles: harusame, fine cellophane noodles made from mung beans whose Japanese name means 'spring rain'; soba, brown buckwheat noodles; somen, fine wheatflour noodles, sometimes flavoured with green tea; udon, thick, white wheatflour noodles.

Pickles: sudori shoga, pickled ginger, traditionally eaten with sushi; takuan, pickled daikon, often bright yellow in colour.

Ponzu: a citric vinegar, often made from the dai dai fruit.

Potato starch (kataturika): strongly binding sweet potato starch.

Rice: short grain, slightly glutinous rice is the staple. A very sticky glutinous 'sweet rice' is used to make desserts and cakes.

Rice vinegar (su): delicate rice vinegar, used in making sushi.

Sake: rice wine, both drunk and used as a flavouring in cooking.

Sansho: known as 'Japanese pepper' this is the seed of the prickly ash tree.

Seaweeds: kombu, a dark large-leafed seaweed used in making dashi stock; nori, thin green sheets of dried seaweed used for sushi, available untoasted or toasted; wakame, dried lobeleaf seaweed.

Shichimi togarashi: a piquant seven-spice mix containing chilli.

Shiso: the aromatic red or green leaves of the perilla or beefsteak plant, used to add both flavour and colour.

Soya beans: raw soya beans (edaname), available frozen, are a snack food. Dried soya beans (daizu) need long cooking.

Soy sauce (shoyu): Japanese soy sauce, available both dark and light, has a different flavour from Chinese soy sauce. Kikkoman is a reputable shoyu manufacturer.

Trefoil (mitsuba): a leaf herb, often found freeze-dried.

Umeboshi: small, deep red, pickled plums, with a tart flavour.

Warabi: young edible sprouts of bracken, picked before they have uncurled, available dried or vacuum-packed.

Wasabi: a pungent green root, compared to horseradish, available in paste or powder form.

Wheat gluten (fu): wheat gluten forms, often coloured, used rather like croutons in soups and simmered dishes.

Yuzu: an aromatic citrus fruit, used to flavour oil.

JAPANESE GLOSSARY

83

A TRIP TO A MIDDLE EASTERN SUPERMARKET: SIX RECIPES

ZAHTAR FOCACCIA
DUCK AND DRIED LIME STEW
SPICED BARBERRY PILAFF
REENA'S SAFFRON CHICKEN
VENISON QUINCE TAGINE
APRICOT PISTACHIO PUDDING

An abundance of fresh herbs (dill, mint and flat-leaf parsley), piles of fruit (including sweet watermelons, tiny sour cherries and pale green apricots with a delicate sweet flavour), packets of spices such as saffron or dark red sumac and an abundance of dried fruits and nuts (dates, pistachios, cashews, almonds) are the images that come to mind when I think of a Middle Eastern food shop.

There are a number of Middle Eastern foodshops throughout London at which to stock up. Yasar Halim on 493 Green Lanes, N4 (0181-340 8090) is a down-to-earth, well-established Turkish foodshop combining a bakery, greengrocer's, delicatessen and halal meat counter, always bustling with customers. For Persian ingredients visit the row of Iranian foodshops at 345-49a Kensington High Street (across the road from the Commonwealth Institute and down a little way towards Olympia). These include Reza Meat Ltd (0171-603 0924) and Super Bahar (0171-603 5083). Lebanese ingredients can be found at Green Valley, 36 Upper Berkeley Street, W1 (0171-402 7385), warmly recommended by cookery writer Claudia Roden.

Super Bahar

ZAHTAR FOCACCIA

Zahtar is a Lebanese spice mixture, made from thyme, salt, sumac and sometimes roasted sesame seeds. Traditionally used on Lebanese breads, here it adds an aromatic flavour to olive oil-rich, salty focaccia bread.

Serve the bread with a platter of antipasti such as cold meats, shallots agrodolce (scalded, then cooked in a sweet and sour dressing), pickled artichoke hearts and a refreshing rocket salad for a delicious meal. Alternatively, use the bread for luxury panini, filled with parma ham, pepperonata and slices of buffalo mozzarella.

Ingredients (serves four to six)

1 tsp sugar
2 tsp dried yeast
300 ml/½ pt hand-hot water
500 g/1 lb 2 oz strong white plain flour
1 tsp salt
8 tbsp extra virgin olive oil
2 tsp coarse sea salt
2 tsp zahtar

Mix sugar into 150 ml/¼ pt hand-hot water. Sprinkle over dried yeast. Leave to stand for 10-15 minutes until a good frothy head forms.

Sift flour into mixing bowl. Pour in remaining 150 ml/¼ pt hand-hot water, 1 tsp salt and 2 tbsp olive oil. Mix together to form a dough. Knead for ten minutes until supple. Cover dough with a clean damp tea-towel and set aside for 1 hour until dough risen and doubled in size.

Knead risen dough briefly. Place on an oiled baking sheet and press out into a large oval about 1 cm/½ in thick. Make indentations in the dough with your fingertips. Pour over 3 tbsp olive oil, spreading it evenly over the surface. Sprinkle over coarse sea salt and zahtar. Set aside to rest for a further 30 minutes.

Preheat oven to Gas Mark 9/240C/475F. Bake for between 15 and 20 minutes until golden-brown. Drizzle over remaining 3 tbsp olive oil and serve warm from the oven.

DUCK AND DRIED LIME STEW

There are a growing number of Iranian restaurants in London, offering delicious Persian food at very reasonable prices. One of my favourite dishes at these restaurants is the khoresht-e gheimeh, a lamb and split pea stew flavoured with limoo or dried limes.

Packets of these small, brown hard limes can be found in Iranian foodshops. Their unremarkable appearance is deceptive as they add a wonderful distinctive fragrance to dishes. Here, I've used duck – a rich, fatty meat – in an unorthodox but successful version of the khoresht-e gheimeh. Serve the stew with rice and a side-vegetable such as green beans or spinach.

Ingredients (serves four)

2 onions
4 duck breast fillets
4 tomatoes
1 tbsp olive oil
1 tsp ground turmeric
2 tbsp tomato puree
300 ml/½ pt chicken stock
4 dried limes
salt and freshly ground pepper

Dried Limes

Peel and finely chop onions. Cut duck into even-sized cubes. Scald tomatoes, then peel and chop them.

Heat olive oil in a casserole dish. Fry chopped onion over medium heat until it begins to brown. Add the duck and brown. Reduce heat, mix in turmeric and cook gently for a couple of minutes. Mix in the tomato puree, chopped tomatoes and chicken stock. Rinse the dried limes and pierce them several times with a sharp knife or skewer to let their full flavour come out, then add into casserole dish. Season with salt and freshly ground pepper. Bring to the boil, reduce heat, cover and simmer for 30 minutes, stirring now and then.

MIDDLE EASTERN

SPICED BARBERRY PILAFF

S mall dark red dried zereshk or barberries (which look like dried redcurrants) add a refreshing tanginess to a number of Persian dishes. Both the barberries and the pistachio slivers can be found in Iranian foodshops.

This colourful and aromatic pilaff would go well with any number of meat, fish or vegetable dishes, or a free-range roast chicken.

Ingredients (serves four)

20 saffron strands
3 tbsp warm water
225 g/8 oz basmati rice
25 g/1 oz dried zereshk (barberries)
2 tbsp ghee
25 g/1 oz pistachio slivers
3 cardamom pods
1 cinnamon stick
400 ml/14 fl oz water
salt

Set the saffron strands to soak in warm water. Rinse the basmati rice throughly to wash out excess starch. Sort through the barberries, picking off any stems and rinse them.

Heat the ghee in a heavy-bottomed saucepan. Gently fry the pistacho nuts, barberries, cardamom pods and cinnamon stick for 2-3 minutes. Mix in the basmati rice. Pour in the saffron water (strands and all) and 400 ml/14 fl oz water. Season with salt.

Bring to the boil. Reduce heat, cover tightly and simmer gently until water is absorbed and rice cooked through.

REENA'S SAFFRON CHICKEN

This dish is a family favourite, eaten in Reena Suleman's family to celebrate special occasions, such as Id at the end of Ramadan. Reena (whose father was Turkish and mother Egyptian) and her family enjoy the chicken with potatoes, vegetables and pitta bread.

Saffron is one of Reena's favourite spices; "I get through it at a rate of knots." She prefers saffron strands to powder as she finds them "more flavourful" and also less likely to be adulterated. Luckily, given the cost of saffron over here, her brother stocks up with it on business trips to the Middle East.

Ingredients (serves ten)

1 kg/2 lb 4 oz chicken breast fillets
5 cm/2 in root ginger
2 cloves garlic
3 onions
2 green chillies
200 ml/7 fl oz of 3 lemon juice
150 ml/½ cup plain yogurt
2 tsp ground caraway seeds
1½ tsp ground coriander
½ tsp ground cinnamon
1 tsp saffron strands
1 tbsp Worcester or soy sauce
1 tsp salt
1 tsp English mustard powder
1 tsp saffron/turmeric powder
25 g/1 oz butter
1 tbsp oil
a few sprigs of fresh coriander

Wash the chicken breast fillets, drain and set aside. Peel and chop the root ginger, garlic and two onions. De-stem and chop green chillies.

Blend together the ginger, garlic, onion, green chillies, 1 tsp lemon juice, yogurt, ground caraway, coriander, cinnamon, saffron strands, Worcester sauce, salt and mustard powder into a paste.

Place the chicken breast fillets in a large bowl. Add in remaining lemon juice and 1 tsp saffron or turmeric powder and mix thoroughly. Add in the blended yogurt paste and mix well, making sure the chicken is well-coated in it. Cover and marinate overnight in the fridge.

Preheat the oven to Gas Mark 5/375F/190C. Spread out the chicken pieces on a baking tray, dot with butter, cover with foil and bake for 1-1½ hours until cooked through and golden-brown.

Meanwhile peel and chop the remaining onion. Fry in oil until browned. Chop fresh coriander. Garnish cooked chicken with fried onion and chopped coriander and serve.

Saffron

VENISON QUINCE TAGINE

I n the autumn months rock-hard yellow quinces, looking like large lumpy pears covered with a soft down, appear in Middle Eastern foodstores and Cypriot greengrocers. Too sour to be eaten raw, quinces add a distinctive fragrance to cooked dishes, both sweet and savoury, taking on a delicate orange-pink colour in the process. According to Jane Grigson's *Fruit Book* the quince was also known as Aphrodite's apple, which is no doubt why that romantic couple Edward Lear's Owl and Pussycat dined on 'mince and slices of quince' to celebrate their marriage.

This recipe is adapted from Claudia Roden's recipe for a Moroccan Tagine with Quince in her seminal *Middle Eastern Food* (a must-have for anyone interested in Middle Eastern cookery) and uses venison instead of lamb. Serve it with couscous or rice.

Ingredients (serves four)

2 onions
1 bunch of flat-leaf parsley
2 tbsp oil
700 g/1½ lb diced venison
water
1 tbsp tomato puree
1 tsp ground ginger
½ tsp ground paprika
½ tsp ground cayenne pepper
salt and freshly ground pepper
1 quince

Peel and finely chop the onions. Finely chop flat-leaf parsley.

Heat the oil in a casserole dish. Gently fry the onions until softened. Add in the venison and brown quickly. Pour in water to cover the meat. Mix in tomato puree, ginger, paprika and cayenne. Season with salt and freshly ground pepper.

Bring to the boil and skim off any skum. Reduce heat, cover and simmer gently for 1 hour. Rub the down off the quince, core and chop it. Add the chopped quince to the tagine and simmer gently for a further ½ hour.

MIDDLE EASTERN

APRICOT PISTACHIO PUDDING

S yrup-soaked pastries are a classic sweet with which to round off a Middle Eastern meal. Here, instead of the more familiar filo a fine white vermicelli-like pastry called konafa (kadaif) is used. This is sold frozen or, more rarely, fresh in Middle Eastern and Cypriot foodstores.

Dried apricots add a pleasant chewiness to the traditional nut filling. Unsulphured dried apricots (sold in healthfood shops) have a particular sweetness and flavour which makes them well worth hunting out.

Ingredients (serves eight)

175 g/6 oz unsalted butter
375 g/13 oz konafa (kadaif)
115 g/4 oz unsulphured pitted dried apricots
150 g/5 oz pistachio slivers
100 g/3 ½ oz ground almonds
¼ tsp ground cardamom

Sugar syrup

450 g/1 lb granulated sugar
250 ml/9 fl oz water
1 tbsp lemon juice
1 tbsp rose/orange flower water

Melt the butter and allow to cool. In a large mixing bowl mix the melted butter into the konafa with your hands, making sure the pastry strands are thoroughly coated.

Chop the dried apricots. Mix together dried apricots, pistachio slivers, ground almonds and cardamom.

Preheat oven to Gas Mark 4/350F/180C. Place half the konafa in a 20 cm/8 in heatproof dish, spreading it out to cover the bottom of the dish. Place the dried apricot mixture in the centre of the konafa and spread it out evenly, leaving a little rim of konafa round the edge. Top with remaining konafa.

Bake the konafa for ½ hour. Increase the heat to Gas Mark 6/400F/200C. Bake for 5-10 minutes until pale gold. Allow to cool.

While the konafa is baking make the sugar syrup. Place the sugar, water and lemon juice in a saucepan. Bring to the boil and cook for around ten minutes until it forms a thick syrup. Remove from heat and mix in rose water. Cool, then chill until needed.

Just before serving pour the sugar syrup over the konafa.

RECOMMENDED COOKBOOKS

Lebanese Cuisine,
Anissa Helou.
An authoritative and appetising look at Lebanese food.

The Legendary Cuisine of Persia,
Margaret Shaida.
An elegantly-written, knowledgeable book charting the history of Persian cuisine, filled with wonderful recipes.

The New Book of Middle Eastern Food,
Claudia Roden.
Written as a labour of love, this is an invaluable and classic book on Middle Eastern cookery, evocatively and authoritatively written and filled with tempting recipes.

MIDDLE E ASTERN

MIDDLE EASTERN GLOSSARY

Allspice: round berry, similar to peppercorns, with a flavour of nutmeg, cinnamon and cloves.

Apricot paste sheets (amretin): translucent orange sheets made from apricots which, when diluted with water, make a refreshing drink. Especially popular during the fasting month of Ramadan.

Barberries (zereshk): tart, red berries, used dried in Iranian cooking to add colour and flavour.

Burghul (bulgar): parboiled, cracked grains of wheat, available both coarse or finely ground.

Coriander: a flat-leafed green herb, similar to continental parsley but with a distinctive sharp taste.

Couscous: fine yellow cereal made from semolina.

Dibbis: thick, dark brown syrup made from dates.

Dill: a caraway-scented herb with fine, feathery green fronds.

Dried limes (limoo): hard, brown, dried limes, used to add a distinctive flavour to Iranian and Iraqi soups and stews.

Filo: paper-thin fine pastry usually found frozen but occasionally available fresh.

Harissa: a fiery, red pimento paste.

Kashk: stony lumps of pungent-smelling dried buttermilk, used in soups and stews. Also available in powdered form.

Konafa (kadaif): a vermicelli-like dough, white in its raw state but resembling shredded wheat once cooked.

Labne (lebne): thick, strained concentrated yogurt, usually sold bottled, shaped into balls, floating in oil.

Mahlab: small pale brown seeds which are the kernels of blackcherry stones, with a spicy fragrance.

Melokhia: a green, leafy vegetable, similar in appearance to mallow, used in making a famous eponymous Egyptian soup. Fresh melokhia is sometimes found, while dried is readily available.

Okra: tapering, ridged green pods, available fresh, dried, tinned or frozen.

Onion seeds (sharmar): small, black teardrop-shaped seeds, not related to onions!

Orange–flower water: a fragrant flavouring made from orange flower essence, used in sweets, drinks and desserts.

Pine nuts: small, ivory-coloured kernels, with the fine, long Lebanese pine nuts being particularly prized.

Pistachio: a small, green-coloured nut, indigenous to Iran.

Pomegranate syrup: made from the concentrated juice of sour pomegranates and used in Iranian cooking.

Pulses: black-eyed beans, with characteristic black markings; chickpeas, rounded yellow peas; Egyptian brown beans (ful): small brown broad beans.

Quince: a hard-yellow skinned fruit, resembling a large, craggy pear. Usually cooked, whereupon its flesh turns pink.

Rice: long-grain rice is a Middle-Eastern staple. Fine-quality Iranian rice is hard to get over here, with Basmati rice being the closest substitute.

Rose water: an essential scented flavouring made from rose-essence and used in sweets and desserts.

Saffron: a costly spice made from the stigmas of a particular crocus variety, sold in thread or powdered form.

Tahini: sesame-seed paste.

Tamarind: a brown pod with sour, dark brown, pulpy flesh and seeds. Available in de-seeded pulp form or as a paste. Also used to make a syrup, which is then diluted into a refreshing drink.

Turmeric: an orange-fleshed rhizome, usually sold in its ground form as a yellow-orange powder. It has a harsh, flat taste and is used to add flavour and a distinctive yellow colour to dishes.

Vine leaves: large, distinctively-shaped leaves of the vine. Occasionally found fresh, but more usually sold in packets, preserved in brine, when they then require soaking in water.

Yogurt: tangy sheep's and goat's yogurt as well as cow's yogurt is widely used in Middle-Eastern cooking.

Zahtar: a spice mix made from thyme, salt, sumac and sometimes roasted sesame seeds, often baked on the top of breads.

A TRIP TO A POLISH DELI: THREE RECIPES

BLINIS
BIGOS
CURD CHEESE POPPYSEED PANCAKES

D espite the fact that London houses a large Polish community, many of whom came over during or after WWII, Polish cuisine remains relatively unknown outside the community. Culinary delights to be found in a Polish deli include excellent rye breads, wonderful cakes, pierogi (or Polish ravioli) and a mind-boggling range of sausages and cured meats to satisfy the traditional Polish love of meat.

There are a number of Polish delis dotted round London with the majority in West London, the traditional home to the Polish community. Among these the well-established Korona Delicatessen, now in smart new premises at 30 Streatham High Road, SW16 (0181-769 6647), continues to attract a steady stream of regular customers. Run by Peter and Elonora Wicinska, this is a favourite Polish foodshop of mine, with courteous, helpful staff and an excellent range of Polish foodstuffs including fabulous poppyseed cheesecake and more-ish plum jam doughnuts.

Korona Delicatessen

BLINIS

Buckwheat is a much-loved grain in Poland, used in kashas (gruels). Buckwheat flour (sold in Polish delis and healthfood shops) gives these tiny yeasty pancakes a distinctive colour and flavour.

Served with any one of the suggested accompaniments blinis make a rich and luxurious meal, one which I would wash down with an icy-cold Polish vodka such as zubrowska (buffalo grass).

Ingredients (serves four as a main course or eight as a starter)

2 eggs
40 g/1½oz butter
1 tsp sugar
300 ml/½pt hand-hot milk
1 tsp dried yeast
150 g/5 oz plain white flour
75 g/3 oz buckwheat flour
1 tsp salt

Suggested accompaniments

Buckwheat

Smoked salmon, soured cream topped with finely chopped chives and lemon wedges
Caviar, salmon roe or lumpfish roe and soured cream topped with finely chopped dill
Smoked undyed haddock, beetroot salad and soured cream
An assortment of pickled herrings

Separate the eggs. Melt the butter. Mix sugar into the hand-hot milk. Sprinkle yeast into the milk. Stir briefly and leave to stand for 10-15 minutes until a frothy head forms.

Meanwhile sift the white flour, buckwheat flour and salt into a warmed mixing bowl. Pour in the yeast mixture. Add egg yolks and mix together to form a thick smooth batter. Stir in melted butter.

Cover and set aside for 1 hour. Beat egg whites until stiff. Genlty fold egg whites into batter with a metal spoon.

Lightly oil a large frying pan or griddle. Heat the pan until very hot. Fry the blinis in batches, using a generous tablespoon of the batter for each one. Fry the blinis until small bubbles appear on the surface and the edges darken, then turn over and briefly brown the other side. Remove to a warmed plate and repeat the process until all the batter has been used up, making around 24 blinis.

BIGOS

A rich combination of slow-cooked meat and sauerkraut, this is a famous Polish dish, known also as Polish Huntsman's Stew. There are innumerable versions of bigos: some include wine and tomato puree or add in cooking apple, while yet another might have garlic but not onion or prunes.

Personally I think the secret of success is to have a high ratio of meat to sauerkraut, around 2:1. One English friend who first encountered a rather lacklustre bigos in a Polish cafe complained "It was rather as if all the huntsman had shot was a cabbage!" Essential to an authentic flavour is that the meat should include some Polish sausages (such as zywiecka and tuchowska) and the smoked streaky Polish bacon called boczek. Jars of sauerkraut are another key Polish ingredient.

You need to plan ahead if you're making bigos as ideally it is heated through and eaten a day after it's been made to allow the flavours to develop.

Serve the bigos with baked or mashed potatoes for a hearty meal.

Ingredients (serves six)

10 g/¼oz dried ceps	*1 tbsp oil*
2 onions	*250 g/9 oz pre-soaked pitted prunes*
454 g jar of sauerkraut	*6 allspice berries*
280 g/10 oz Polish bacon (boczek)	*1 tsp caraway seeds*
350 g/12 oz Polish sausages	*chicken stock/water*
(zywiecka and tuchowska)	*freshly ground pepper*
450 g/1 lb boneless shoulder of pork	

Soak the ceps in a little warm water for 20 minutes. Drain (straining and reserving the cep water) and chop the ceps. Peel and finely chop onions. Rinse the sauerkraut in cold water and drain.

Trim the skin off the Polish bacon and cube. Cut the zywiecka, tuchowska and boneless shoulder of pork into 2.5 cm/1 in pieces.

Heat the oil in a large, heavy-bottomed casserole dish. Fry the onion until it begins to brown. Add in the bacon, sausages and pork and fry until browned, stirring often. Add in the chopped ceps, reserved cep water, prunes, sauerkraut, allspice and caraway. Pour over enough stock to just cover the ingredients.

Bring to the boil, reduce heat, cover and simmer for 2 hours, stirring now and then. Allow to cool and store in the fridge overnight.

Gently reheat for a further hour, stirring often. By the end of this last hour most of the liquid should have evaporated, leaving a thick, meltingly soft mass of sauerkraut and meat. Season with freshly ground pepper and serve.

CURD CHEESE POPPYSEED PANCAKES

Poppyseeds are a key ingredient in Polish baking, sold in 450 g/1 lb bags rather than the little 100 g sachets one finds in British supermarkets. In the run-up to Christmas Korona delicatessen does a roaring trade in prepared poppyseeds (crushed and flavoured with honey) ready to use in baking.

These subtly crunchy pancakes enclose a traditional curd cheese filling and make a delicious, rich dessert.

Ingredients (serves four)

Pancakes

115 g/4 oz plain flour
pinch of salt
1 egg
300 ml/½ pt milk
1 tbsp brandy
40 g/1½ oz blue poppyseeds
butter for frying

Curd cheese filling

1 egg
350 g/¾ lb curd cheese
2 tbsp vanilla sugar
grated zest of 1 lemon
25 g/1 oz sultanas
1 tbsp sour cream

Sift the flour and salt into a mixing bowl. Break in the egg and gradually beat in the milk to make a thick, smooth batter. Mix in the brandy. Cover and leave to stand for an hour. Mix in the poppyseeds.

Heat a little butter in a 23 cm/9 in frying pan. Pour in a ladleful of the pancake batter, tilting the pan to spread it evenly. Fry until set and the edges begin to curl up, then turn and cook briefly on the other side. Remove pancake to a plate and repeat process making eight pancakes in all. Set aside to cool.

To make the filling first separate the egg. Beat together the curd cheese, egg yolk, vanilla sugar and lemon zest. Mix in sultanas and sour cream. Whisk the egg white until stiff and fold in.

Spread each pancake with a portion of the curd cheese mixture. Fold the pancakes over into quarters. Heat a little butter in a large frying pan and fry the filled pancakes quickly until golden-brown on each side. Serve while warm.

RECOMMENDED COOKBOOKS

The Food and Cooking of Eastern Europe,
Leslie Chamberlain.
A clearly-written, overall look at East European cookery.

The Polish Kitchen,
Mary Pininska.
A well-written, knowledgeable book on Polish cookery with appetising recipes.

POLISH GLOSSARY

Buckwheat: a triangular brown-green grain. Buckwheat flour is used in blinis.

Cakes: Cakes and pastries are an important feature of Polish life, and a huge variety is made, some traditionally eaten at Christmas and Easter. Babka, a famous Easter yeast cake with a distinctive fluted shape; cheesecake, traditionally baked and not oversweet; makowiec, poppy-seed roll; mazurek, flat, traditionally rectangular cakes eaten at Easter; paczki, Polish doughnuts, often filled with plum jam.

Caraway seeds: tiny, ridged brown seeds, with an aniseed flavour.

Curd cheese: a slightly tangy soft cheese made from curds, used in pierogi and cheesecake.

Dill: a caraway-flavoured herb with delicate, feathery fronds.

Dried mushrooms: hunting for wild mushrooms is a national pastime in Poland. Fresh wild mushrooms are rarely found in the shops, but both dried and pickled mushrooms are widely available.

Juniper berries: aromatic, blue-black berries, used with game.

Kohlrabi: a plump, rounded vegetable, either pale green or deep purple, called a 'cabbage-turnip' by Jane Grigson.

Pierogi: filled pasta pouches, often called Polish ravioli.

Pinhead barley: fine-grained barley.

Polish pure spirit: a powerful spirit, 168 proof, used to make vodka.

Poppy seeds: tiny white or purple-blue seeds, used in vast quantities in Polish baking.

Rye bread: a Polish fundamental. Rich-flavoured, dark brown Ukranian rye is distinctive.

Sauerkraut: pickled, shredded cabbage with a sharp flavour, available fresh or bottled.

Sausages: boiling ring, loops of spicy sausages; kabanos, long, thin pork sausages; kielbasa, pork and beef sausage flavoured with garlic; krakowska, garlic sausage, eaten as a salami.

A TRIP TO A PORTUGUESE OR SPANISH DELI: SIX RECIPES

QUINCE JELLY CHEESE TOASTIES
MICHAEL'S CALDO VERDE
SALT COD FISHCAKES WITH PARSLEY PESTO
CHORIZO-STUFFED ROAST CHICKEN
SERRANO HAM MONKFISH KEBABS
PAELLA

The tapas bar boom during the 1980s means that Spanish ingredients such as chorizo sausage or jamon Serrano have become more familiar than they once were. Portuguese cuisine, however, remains less well-known despite the cult status of Lisboa Patisserie's delectable custard tarts, now sold at a number of discerning coffee bars.

The area around Notting Hill is a fruitful ground for those searching for Iberian delicacies, with the large veteran Spanish foodstore Garcia R & Sons at 248 Portobello Road, W11 (0171-221 6119) and London's first Portuguese delicatessen Lisboa (across the road from the Patisserie) at 54 Golborne Road, W10 (0181-969 1052). More centrally Products from Spain at 89 Charlotte Street, W1 (0171-580 2905) has an excellent range of Spanish foodstuffs, supplying as it does a number of tapas bars and Spanish restaurants.

Garcia R. & Sons

QUINCE JELLY CHEESE TOASTIES

Packets of golden membrillo or marmelada (a thick jelly-like fruit 'cheese' made from quinces) can be found in both Portuguese and Spanish delis. Traditionally, it is eaten as an accompaniment to cheese. Here I've taken that idea one step further to make delicious cheese toasties, with the honey-sweetness of the membrillo coming through a salty layer of cheese. Rather extravagantly I've suggested mature manchego (a Spanish ewe's milk cheese sold according to age) but one could substitute a good mature Cheddar.

Ingredients (serves four)

225 g/8 oz membrillo (quince jelly)
225 g/8 oz mature manchego cheese
4 large slices of good bread

Finely slice the membrillo (quince jelly) and manchego cheese.
Lightly toast the bread on both sides. Top one side with a layer of membrillo and then a layer of manchego cheese. Grill until the cheese has melted and serve at once.

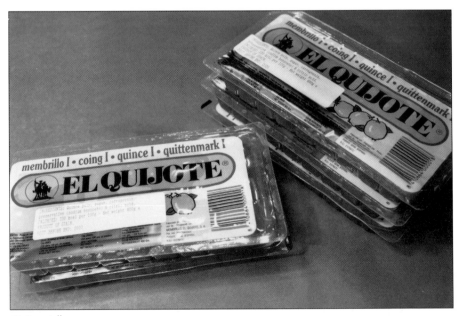

Quince Jelly

MICHAEL'S CALDO VERDE

Michael Rimmer is an open-minded and adventurous cook and dedicated eater-out. He returns from holidays abroad with an array of goodies for his kitchen, whether it be Portuguese crockery or a bread-maker from Hong Kong.

This is his version of a hearty Portuguese soup, simple but very satisfying. Chourico or chorizo (paprika sausage) can be found in Portuguese or Spanish delicatessens and adds a distinctive flavour to the soup. Michael suggests serving it with bread and wine for a comforting winter supper.

Ingredients (serves six)

2 lb potatoes
3 cloves garlic
1 onion
280 g/10 oz chourico/chorizo
700 g/1½ lb Savoy cabbage
4 tbsp extra virgin olive oil
1.7 ltr/3 pt good chicken or vegetable stock
salt and freshly ground pepper
6 tbsp chopped flat-leaf parsley

Peel the potatoes and chop into large pieces. Peel and finely chop the garlic and onion. Cut the chourico into slices about ½ cm/¼ in thick. Strip the tough outer leaves from the cabbage, then cut it in half and remove the stalk and core, cutting them out in a V shape. Finely shred the cabbage leaves.

Heat 2 tbsp of the olive oil in a frying pan over a low heat. Add the onion and garlic and cook until softened and onion translucent. Set aside.

Place chopped potatoes and stock in a large saucepan. Bring to the boil. Reduce the heat and simmer for 15-20 minutes. Mash the cooked potatoes and stock together in the saucepan to a smooth consistency. Season with salt and freshly ground pepper. Add in the fried onion and garlic, sliced chorizo and shredded cabbage. Simmer until all the ingredients are warmed through. Check the seasoning.

Decant into six deep soup bowls. Drizzle remaining extra virgin olive oil over each helping and scatter with a tbsp of chopped flat-leaf parsley.

SALT COD FISHCAKES WITH PARSLEY PESTO

H uge slabs of rock-hard, salt-encrusted salt cod (bacalhau in Portuguese or bacalao in Spanish) are among the traditional foodstuffs on sale in Portuguese and Spanish delis.

Cooking salt cod involves planning in advance as it needs to be soaked for several hours to both soften it and remove the excess salt. Mixed with potato it makes delicious fishcakes with a subtle but distinctive flavour, set off by the pleasant sweetness of the parsley pesto.

Ingredients (serves four)

380 g/13 oz salt cod (bacalhau or bacalao)
450 g/1 lb potatoes
salt and freshly ground pepper
1 clove garlic
1 spring onion
1 egg
2 tbsp fine breadcrumbs/matzo meal
oil for shallow-frying

Parsley pesto

55 g/2 oz pine nuts
25 g/1 oz grated Parmesan
55 g/2 oz flat-leaf parsley
6 tbsp extra virgin olive oil

Cover the salt cod with cold water and set aside to soak for 36 hours, changing the water every six to eight hours. Drain the soaked cod and add to a saucepan of boiling water, cooking it over a medium heat for 20 minutes; drain. When cool enough to handle, finely flake the salt cod with your fingers, discarding any skin or bones.

Peel and quarter the potatoes. Add the potatoes to a saucepan of salted boiling water. Reduce heat and cook gently until tender; drain and mash.

Peel and crush garlic. Trim and finely chop spring onion, both white and green parts. Mix together the flaked salt cod, mashed potato, crushed garlic, chopped spring onion and egg into a smooth puree. Season with freshly ground pepper. Shape into eight small fishcakes. Roll fishcakes in breadcrumbs or matzo meal, coating thoroughly.

Make the parsley pesto by finely grinding the pine nuts. Blend together ground pine nuts, grated Parmesan cheese, flat-leaf parsley and olive oil into a smooth green paste.

Heat the oil in a large frying pan. Fry the salt cod fishcakes until golden-brown on both sides. Serve hot from the pan with a dollop of parsley pesto.

CHORIZO-STUFFED ROAST CHICKEN

This is a tasty variation on the traditional roast chicken. Chorizo or chourico (paprika sausages) can be found in Spanish or Portuguese delis and make a very tasty stuffing.

Serve the chicken with rice and a selection of vegetables, such as green beans, carrots and mushrooms for a substantial meal.

Ingredients (serves four)

2 cloves garlic
115 g/¼ lb chorizo/chourico sausage
a 1.4 kg/3 lb free-range chicken
salt and freshly ground pepper
2 tbsp pine nuts
3 tbsp medium dry sherry
1 tbsp olive oil

Preheat the oven to Gas Mark 6/400F/200C. Peel and chop the garlic. Roughly chop the chorizo. Season the chicken inside and out with salt and freshly ground pepper.

Mix together garlic, chorizo and pine nuts. Fill the chicken cavity with the chorizo mixture.

Place the chicken on a rack in a roasting tray. Pour over the sherry then brush with olive oil.

Roast for ½ hour, then reduce heat to Gas Mark 5/375F/190C and bake for a further hour. Check that the chicken is cooked through by piercing just behind the leg joint with a skewer and seeing if the juices run clear. If they do, the chicken is ready to serve.

Salt Cod

SERRANO HAM MONKFISH KEBABS

S errano ham, like Italian Parma ham, is a highly-prized salt-cured Spanish ham, delicious eaten finely sliced with 'pan con tomate', slices of good white bread rubbed with a ripe tomato then flavoured with salt and a drizzle of olive oil.

When cooked, as it is in this recipe, the Serrano ham shrinks and becomes deliciously crispy, in pleasant contrast to the tender cubes of monkfish.

Ingredients (serves four)

700 g/1½lb monkfish fillet
1 tbsp lemon juice
2 tbsp olive oil
1 tbsp chopped flat-leaf parsley
freshly ground pepper
1 red onion
1 red pepper
4 slices of Serrano ham
1 lemon
8 bay leaves

Cut the monkfish fillet into 2.5 cm/1 in cubes. Toss together with lemon juice, 1 tbsp olive oil and flat-leaf parsley. Season with freshly ground pepper and set aside.

Peel onion and cut into fine squares. De-seed red pepper and cut into squares. Cut Serrano ham into broad strips. Quarter the lemon.

Preheat grill. Wrap the monkfish cubes in Serrano ham strips. Thread the wrapped monkfish cubes onto four skewers, alternating them with the onion and red pepper squares and bay leaves. Brush with 1 tbsp olive oil.

Grill the monkfish kebabs until cooked, turning them over once while they cook. Serve at once with lemon wedges.

PAELLA

This version of a classic Spanish rice dish makes a spectacular feast for family and friends. Spicy chorizo sausages, rounded paella rice (which like risotto rice absorbs large amounts of liquid) and saffron can be found in Spanish delis as can paellera, the large flat pans in which paella is cooked.

Ingredients (serves six to eight)

1 red pepper	1 ltr/1¾pt good chicken stock
2 onions	½tsp ground saffron
2 cloves garlic	4 tbsp olive oil
4 chicken breast fillets	2 bay leaves
2 spicy chorizo	400 g/14 oz paella rice
175 g/6 oz green beans	150 ml/¼pt dry white wine
2 lemons	8 raw tiger prawns
1 medium squid, cleaned	4 tbsp chopped flat-leaf parsley
16 clams or mussels	salt and freshly ground pepper

Grill the red pepper until charred all over. Wrap in a plastic bag (this makes it easier to peel) and set aside to cool. Once cool, peel, de-seed and chop into long strips.

Peel and chop onions and garlic. Cube chicken breast fillets. Chop chorizo into chunks. Top and tail green beans and cut into short lengths. Cut lemons into wedges. Chop the squid body into rings and the tendrils into short pieces. Wash and sort through the clams, discarding any that are cracked or open. Keep in the fridge until needed.

In a large saucepan bring the chicken stock to a rolling boil. Add in the saffron. Heat the olive oil in a 28 cm/11 in paella pan or heavy-bottomed frying pan. Fry the onion, garlic and bay leaves until fragrant. Add the chicken and chorizo and fry until chicken whitened. Add in the squid and green beans and cook, stirring often, until squid whitened. Mix in the rice and stir well, coating it with the oil.

Pour in the boiling stock and white wine. Mix in the prawns, clams and parsley. Season with salt and freshly ground pepper. Bring to the boil and cook over high heat for around 10 minutes. Reduce the heat and simmer for a further ten minutes until stock absorbed and rice tender. Decorate with the red pepper strips. Cover with a silver foil 'lid' and set aside to rest for 5 minutes. Serve with lemon wedges.

RECOMMENDED COOKBOOKS

The Food of Spain and Portugal,
Elizabeth Lambert Ortiz,
A knowledgeable look at Iberian cooking with accessible recipes.

The Foods and Wines of Spain,
Penelope Casas.
An excellent comprehensive and appetising survey of Spanish cuisine.

The Spanish Kitchen,
Nicholas Butcher.
Entertainingly written with a strong emphasis on the regional diversity of Spanish cuisine.

The Taste of Portugal,
Edite Vieira.
A knowledgeable, detailed look at Portuguese cuisine, with appetising, well-written recipes.

PORTUGUESE & SPANISH GLOSSARY

Anchovies (boquerones, biqueiros): tiny cured fish, usually filleted, with a strong, salty flavour.

Capers (alcaparras): the unopened buds of a Mediterranean shrub, sold and used in their pickled form. Spain is the world's largest caper producer.

Cava: sparkling Spanish wine made by the champagne method, with Cordoniu and Frexenet among the best producers.

Charcuterie: butifarra, a white Spanish sausage, spiced with cinnamon, cloves and nutmeg; chorizo/chourico, a range of paprika sausages, used in cooked dishes, to which they add a distinctive colour and flavour, or eaten as a salami; jamon de Serrano, a highly prized, salt-cured Spanish ham, the best of which is made from the acorn-fed pigs of the Estremadura region; lomo, cured pork loin from Spain; presunto, a fine salt-cured ham from Portugal, traditionally made from acorn-fed pigs from Tras-os-Montes.

Cheese: azeitaio, small Portuguese sheep's milk cream cheeses; cabrales, a famous Spanish blue-veined cheese, made from cow's milk and sometimes with sheep's or goat's milk added; evora, a creamy, strong, salty sheep's milk cheese from Portugal; idiazabal, a much-prized, semi-soft cheese with a dark rind made from sheep's milk in the Basque region of Spain; ilha, a Portuguese Cheddar-like cheese made from cow's milk; mahon, a flavourful Spanish semi-soft cow's milk cheese; manchego, one of Spain's best-known cheeses, made with sheep's milk and sold in three grades depending on age; roncal, a hard, Spanish, sheep's milk cheese; serra, a soft, Portuguese, sheep's milk cheese.

Chickpeas (garbanzos, grado): hazelnut-shaped, yellow peas.

Coriander (coentros): a sharp-flavoured green herb, similar in appearance to continental parsley, widely used in Portuguese cookery.

Madeira: a famous Portuguese fortified wine, from the island of Madeira.

Madelenas: small, sweet, golden-brown cakes, eaten for breakfast in Spain.

Olive oil: olive oil is produced in both Spain and Portugal and is the main cooking oil in both countries. Carbonell, with its elegant Art Nouveau labels, is one of Spain's famous brands.

Olives: green olives stuffed with anchovies are particularly popular in Spain.

Paprika: a bright red powder, made from ground sweet or spicy peppers and used as a spice.

Pine kernels (pinon, pinhao): small, ivory-coloured stone pine kernels, used in both sweet and savoury dishes.

Piri piri: a hot Portuguese sauce made from chillies, a culinary legacy from Portugal's colonial past.

Port: a fortified wine from the Douro valley in north-west Portugal. Its creation is traced back to the early seventeenth century when, due to Anglo-French hostilities, Portuguese wine rather than French claret was exported to England.

Quince paste (membrillo, marmelo): a thick, golden, jelly-like paste made from quinces, eaten as a sweetmeat or as a classic accompaniment for cheese.

Saffron: a costly spice made from the stigmas of a type of crocus, sold in either thread or powdered form.

Salt cod (bacalao, bacalhau): dried, salted cod traditionally eaten on Fridays for religious reasons. In Portugal it is regarded as a national delicacy and there is said to be a different bacalhau recipe for every day of the year. It should be soaked for 24–36 hours before cooking to remove excess salt.

Sherry: a classic Spanish wine named after the town of Jerez and imported by the British since the 15th century.

Tiger nut (chufa): a small, wrinkled rhizome from which horchata, a refreshing almond-flavoured drink thought to have been introduced by the Moors, is made.

Turron: Spanish nougat, available in two forms: alicante, crisp and textured with chopped nuts or jijona, soft and crumbly, made from ground nuts. Traditionally this is a Christmas treat but it is now available all the year round.

PORTUGUESE & SPANISH GLOSSARY

A TRIP TO IKEA:
ONE RECIPE

Tucked away among the sofas, desks and kitchen units on Ikea's first floor is a small food section. Homesick Swedes travel round the North Circular to Ikea to stock up here with the essentials of Swedish cuisine: huge round crispbreads, ready-made Swedish meatballs and jars of lingonberries.

Lingonberries

ANNA'S SWEDISH HERRING SALAD

SWEDISH

Strongly attached to her Swedish roots, Anna Persson (who has a Swedish mother and an English father) is among those nostalgic Swedes who make regular visits to Ikea, stocking up with wafer-thin spiced biscuits and gingerbread houses at Christmas time, Swedish mustard and tubes of caviar paste.

This recipe is based on traditional Swedish recipes for herring salad; "not one jot original" emphasises Anna. Essential to its flavour is the dill-marinated herring, sold in jars at Ikea. The beetroot turns the salad a bright pink – a colour which always surprises Anna's English friends – however, she says once they've tried it the salad always gets eaten up.

Serve with an assortment of other cold dishes such as smoked salmon, slices of good ham, a bowlful of radishes, tiny meatballs, potato salad and rye bread for a Scandinavian-style summer buffet.

Ingredients (serves four)

3 medium-sized cooked potatoes
2 large dill pickled gherkins
6 pickled baby beetroot
3 crisp eating apples
1 mild onion
275 g jar marinated dill herrings
salt and freshly ground pepper
4 tbsp creme fraiche
2 tbsp Dijon mustard

Finely dice the potatoes, gherkins and beetroot. De-core apples and finely dice. Peel and finely chop onion. Cut the dill herrings into little dice. According to Anna the secret of success is to cut the ingredients "into neat little dolly-mixture size cubes".

Mix together the chopped potato, gherkins, beetroot, apple, onion and herring. Season with salt and freshly ground pepper.

Mix together the creme fraiche and Dijon mustard. Stir into herring mixture, mixing well. Cover and chill until serving.

A TRIP TO A THAI SUPERMARKET: TEN RECIPES

POMELO PRAWN SALAD
THAI GREEN CHICKEN CURRY
LIME LEAF MEATBALLS
STIR-FRIED YARD LONG GREEN BEANS
RANU'S RENDANG
RANU'S BALINESE ROAST DUCK
CITRUS COD BANANA LEAF PARCEL
WINGED BEANS IN OYSTER SAUCE
COCONUT ICE CREAM SUNDAE
BLACK RICE PUDDING WITH MANGO

Thailand's popularity as a holiday destination has resulted in a new interest in its delicious cuisine. Although there are Thai restaurants throughout London (many of them in pubs), Thai supermarkets are only to be found in West and South-West London. Of these my personal favourite is Sri Thai at 56 Shepherd's Bush Road, W6 (0171-602 0621) which has good quality ingredients and is run with friendly courtesy by Mr and Mrs Thepprasits. Tuesday is the best day to visit for fresh Thai produce, as it's delivered the night before. Many of the Chinese supermarkets have also responded to demand by stocking Thai ingredients such as kaffir lime leaves, galingale and fish sauce, though not in the range of the specialist Thai shops.

Sri Thai

POMELO PRAWN SALAD

Pomelo, which look like large pale green grapefruit, can be found in Thai and Chinese supermarkets and have a distinctive citrus flavour, much more fragrant than a grapefruit's. If you're interested in Thai cooking then both fish sauce, which looks like watery soy sauce and crunchy pre-cooked fried onion flakes are two store cupboard items well worth investing in.

Distinctly Thai, with its contrasting textures and chilli hotness, this easily-prepared salad makes an excellent first course for a Thai meal.

Ingredients (serves four as a starter)

1 clove garlic
1 shallot
1 red chilli
1 tbsp oil
1 tbsp fish sauce
1 tsbp soft dark brown sugar
2 tbsp lime juice
1 pomelo
225 g/8 oz cooked peeled prawns
2 tbsp fried onion flakes

Peel and finely chop garlic and shallot. De-stem and finely chop chilli. Heat the oil in a small frying pan. Fry the garlic, shallot and chilli until lightly browned. Remove from heat and mix the contents of the frying pan with the fish sauce, sugar and lime juice.

Cut the thick peel and white pith off the pomelo. Cut the flesh into small segments. Place in a dish.

Toss together pomelo, prawns and chilli dressing. Top with onion flakes and serve at once.

THAI GREEN CHICKEN CURRY

T his dish is often what people are thinking of when they say "I love Thai food". It is a classic Thai curry, fiercely hot yet also fragrant and salty-sweet. The recipe is in two stages: first for a quantity of curry paste (which can be stored in the fridge) then for the dish itself which should be served with steamed rice. Once the paste has been made the curry itself is simple to make.

It's well worth tracking down the ingredients at a Thai or Chinese supermarket. Galingale is an aromatic rhizome which looks like a white-pink version of root ginger. It is often stored in the chilled cabinets. Lemon grass is a long citrus-flavoured fibrous stem, generally sold in small bunches. Shrimp paste has an extremely pungent salty fishy smell but don't be put off. When cooked this pungency becomes a subtle and essential bass note. Thai fish sauce has similar properties. The curry itself also contains tinned coconut milk, now widely available, pea aubergines, tiny bitter round aubergines which look like little pale green peas and dark glossy kaffir lime leaves, with their wonderful citrus aroma and flavour.

Ingredients (makes 6-8 tbsp)

Green Curry Paste
½ tsp cumin seeds
½ tsp coriander seeds
8 black peppercorns
1 nutmeg
2 cloves
2 shallots
4 cloves garlic
1½ in/3½ cm piece of galingale
8 small green chillies
2 stalks of lemongrass
1 tsp shrimp paste (kapee)
2 tbsp oil
3 oz/75g fresh coriander, including roots and stalks
grated zest of 1 lime
1 tsp salt

Dry-roast cumin and coriander seeds. Grind together cumin, coriander seeds, peppercorns, nutmeg and cloves. Peel and chop shallots, garlic and galingale. Chop chillies, discarding stems. Peel and discard tough outer leaves from lemon grass. Finely chop lower white bulbous part of the lemon grass, discarding remaining stalk.

Blend together all the spice paste ingredients to form a thick paste. Transfer to a clean, dry container, cover and store in the fridge for up to two months.

117

Thai Green Chicken Curry

Ingredients (serves four)

450 g/1 lb boneless chicken
55 g/2 oz pea aubergines
400 ml tin coconut milk
2 tbsp green curry paste (see p.117)
2 tbsp fish sauce
8 kaffir lime leaves
227 g tin sliced bamboo shoots
1 tbsp palm sugar/dark brown sugar
25 g/1 oz basil leaves
2 red chillies

Cut chicken into small chunks. Prepare pea aubergines by pulling them off their stalks.

Heat a tbsp of the thick coconut cream found at the top of the tin of coconut milk in a casserole dish. Fry the green curry paste until fragrant. Add in the chicken chunks and fry, stirring, until they whiten. Add in the coconut milk. Stirring, bring it to the boil. Reduce the heat to a simmer and add in fish sauce, lime leaves and drained bamboo shoots.

Cook gently for 10 minutes, stirring now and then. Add in the pea aubergines and cook gently for a further 10 minutes. Mix in the palm sugar, basil leaves and red chillies and serve.

LIME LEAF MEATBALLS

Dark green, glossy kaffir lime leaves add a distinctive citrus fragrance to many of the best-known Thai dishes, from Tom Yum Goong (a hot sour prawn soup) to Green Chicken Curry. They are sold in packets (stored in the chilled section) or, more rarely, in large bunches in Thai and Chinese supermarkets. A word of warning – do look out for the very sharp thorns on the branches. I pick the leaves off the branches before storing them to spare myself getting spiked. Any excess of lime leaves can be wrapped well and frozen.

This recipe is for Italian-style meatballs, substituting lime leaves for the fresh lemon leaves which would be used in Italy. The leaves add a subtle but distinctive citrus flavour to the meatballs. Serve with rice and a tomato and coriander salsa.

Ingredients (serves four)

2 cloves garlic
1 spring onion
450 g/1 lb minced lamb
½ tsp freshly grated nutmeg
1 tsp ground cinnamon
1 tsp finely grated lemon zest
salt and freshly ground pepper
40 kaffir lime leaves
a little oil

Peel and finely chop garlic. Trim and finely chop spring onion, both white and green parts.

Mix together minced lamb, garlic, spring onion, nutmeg, cinnamon and lemon zest. Season generously with salt and freshly ground pepper. Shape into small meatballs, about the size of a marble.

Preheat the grill. Thread the meatballs on to skewers, alternating them with the kaffir lime leaves.

Brush with a little oil and grill until cooked through, turning over during the cooking time. Serve warm from the grill.

STIR-FRIED YARD-LONG BEANS WITH PORK

A s their name suggests, these are indeed long green beans, often sold pre-packed in plastic bags in the chilled section. This dish is a classic Thai combination. Both the fish sauce and little jars of deliciously crunchy pre-cooked fried onion flakes can be found in Thai and Chinese supermarkets.

Serve with rice for a quick and simple meal.

Ingredients

350 g/12 oz yard-long beans
4 cloves garlic
1 red chilli
350 g/12 oz pork fillet
2 tbsp groundnut oil
2 tbsp fish sauce
1 tbsp sugar
1 tbsp freshly ground black pepper
1 tbsp fried onion flakes

Top, tail and finely chop yard-long beans. Peel and chop garlic. Chop chilli, discarding stem. Cut pork into short fine strips.

Heat wok. Add oil. Fry garlic until golden. Add pork and stir-fry until whitened. Add in chopped yard-long beans, chilli, fish sauce, sugar and black pepper. Stir-fry for 5 minutes. Sprinkle over onion flakes and serve at once.

Fish Sauce

RANU'S VENISON RENDANG

THAI

Born in Singapore Ranu Dally, together with her husband Chris and son Nikhil, spent many happy years living in Java in Indonesia. During this time they explored the fascinating vast achipelago of islands that form Indonesia, with Ubud in Bali being a particularly much-loved place to which they often return.

A wonderful and adventurous cook, Ranu cooks food from around the world. Having now come to live in England she recreates some of her favourite Indonesian dishes at home, much to her family's delight. Ranu finds the ingredients she needs for the following two dishes at a large Sainsbury's and Wang Thai, a Thai supermarket in Richmond. The latter supplys the galingale, krachai, lemon grass and candlenuts, essential for the dishes' authentic flavour and texture.

Rendang is a classic Indonesian dish, traditionally made with beef cooked very slowly in an aromatic mixture of coconut milk and spices until the liquid has disappeared, leaving a 'dry' dish of intensely-flavoured, sweet-ish tender meat with a chilli kick. With the BSE scare in mind, Ranu substitutes venison for beef very successfully.

For best results the rendang should be made at least a day in advance, then heated through before serving, as this allows the flavours to develop fully.

Serve with rice and a vegetable side-dish such as Rojak (see page 40).

Ingredients (serves six)

1 kg/2 lb 4 oz boneless venison steak	2 heaped tbsp dessicated coconut
275 g/9 ½oz onions	2 tbsp oil
8 fat garlic cloves	1 tsp turmeric powder
20 g/¾oz root ginger	1 heaped tsp chilli powder
20 g/¾oz galingal (lengkuas, laos or khaa)	1 tsp brown sugar
10 g/¼ oz krachai (kencur)	salt
4 lemon grass stalks	400 g/14 oz can of coconut milk
6 candlenuts (kemiri, buah keras)	

Cut the venison into 5 cm/2 in pieces. Peel and chop the onions. Peel and crush the garlic, ginger, galingal and krachai. Crush the bulbous end of the lemon grass stalks. Pound the candlenuts into a paste. In a small frying pan dry-fry the dessicated coconut until browned, stirring often to ensure it doesn't burn.

Heat the oil in a heavy stewing pan or casserole dish until very hot. Quickly brown the venison, sealing in the meat juices. Add in the remaining ingredients except for the browned dessicated coconut.

Bring to the boil, then cover the pan, reduce the heat and simmer for 45 minutes to an hour, stirring occasionally. Test the meat for tenderness; it should be nearly done. Add in the browned dessicated coconut, mixing in well. Continue to cook the dish uncovered so as to let the juices evaporate. Stir it now and then, scraping the bottom of the pan to prevent it burning. When the meat is quite tender and the liquid has evaporated then the rendang is ready. Cool and set aside in the fridge for at least 24 hours. Reheat it and remove the lemon grass stalks before serving.

Lemon Grass

RANU'S BALINESE ROAST DUCK – BETUTU IN A MICROWAVE

As Ranu points out, "A Balinese looking at this dish would have a fit". Traditionally betutu (Balinese roast duck) is made by coating and stuffing a duck with an aromatic paste of spices, herbs and roots, wrapping it in several layers of banana leaves, steaming it, then roasting it on a charcoal fire. The result, says Ranu, "is duck so tender that it falls off the bone and so juicy that it melts in the mouth". Ranu's cooking method may be rather more mundane but the rich, flavourful results are deliciously close to the real betutu. Remember that preparations need to start the day before you serve the dish as it needs to marinate overnight.

On a practical note, check that your microwave will hold a whole duck before embarking on the dish. Alternatively, Ranu suggests using duck pieces if cooking on a smaller scale. For those without a microwave wrap the marinated duck in two layers of greaseproofpaper, steam it for around 1½ hours until cooked, then finish it off in the oven as in the recipe.

Krachai or kencur, also known as lesser galingale, is an aromatic rhizome with little finger-like tubers. This, as well as the lemon grass, kaffir lime leaves and large waxy white candlenuts can be found in Thai supermarkets.

Ranu suggests serving the duck with white rice, a fresh side-salad and a chilli sambal, the recipe for which is given below.

Ingredients (serves four to five)

a 2 kg/4 lb 8 oz oven-ready duck
2 large onions
6 fat garlic cloves
20 g/¾ oz root ginger
20 g/¾ oz krachai (kencur)
3 lemon grass stalks
6 kaffir lime leaves
6 candlenuts (kemiri, buah keras)
3 tbsp oil
1 tsp ground turmeric
1 tsp ground coriander
1 tsp salt
1 tsp coarsely ground black pepper

Chilli Sambal

12 medium-hot red chillies	2 tbsp oil
1 tomato	course sea salt
juice of ½ lemon	fried onion flakes
1 heaped tsp shrimp paste (blachan, terasi or kapi)	
1 scant tsp sugar	

Remove the duck's giblets and trim away excess fat, as Balinese ducks, which lead an active life in the paddy-fields, are far less fatty. Wipe the cavity with kitchen paper.

Peel and chop the onions, garlic, ginger and krachai. Remove tough outer leaves from the lemon grass and chop the lower bulbous part, discarding the tougher upper part of the stalk. Shred the kaffir lime leaves, discarding stalks. Process together the onion, garlic, ginger, krachai, lemon grass, candlenuts and kaffir lime leaves until finely ground.

Mix together the onion paste, oil, turmeric, coriander, salt and black pepper. Now rub this mixture into the duck, inside and out, and stuff the duck with what's left. Wrap the duck in two layers of greaseproof paper, tie with string, and leave it overnight in the fridge.

Loosely wrap the duck bundle with microwave film and cook the duck in the microwave, following the instructions of your particular microwave (usually about 7-9 minutes to the pound).

Meanwhile, preheat your oven to Gas Mark 6/400F/200C. Line a roasting tray with oiled aluminium foil. When the duck has been cooked in the microwave, take it out, unwrap it and carefully transfer it into the lined roasting tray. Using a slotted spoon pick up any remaining spice mixture in the wrapping and spread it over the duck. Cover the duck loosely with foil and roast in the oven for 45 minutes. Remove from oven, allow to stand for about ten minutes, then cut it into serving pieces and place on a serving platter. While the duck is roasting you can cook the rice, prepare the salad and make the sambal (alternately the sambal can be made in advance and will keep for days in an airtight jar in the fridge).

To make the sambal de-stem and halve the red chillies. Blend together chillies, tomato, lemon juice, shrimp paste (blachan, terasi or, in Thai, kapi) and sugar.

Heat 2 tbsp oil in a small frying pan. When the oil is very hot pour in the chilli paste. Allow it to sizzle angrily for half a minute, then reduce the heat and simmer the sambal, stirring now and then, until it becomes a dry pulp and the oil rises to the surface. Remove from heat and let it cool.

To serve the sambal with the duck give each person a small bowl or plate and place on it a little of the chilli sambal, a little coarse sea salt and some fried onion flakes. These are then mixed and eaten with the rice and the duck.

CITRUS COD BANANA LEAF PARCEL

T his recipe uses fresh banana leaf (sold folded in packets in Thai supermarkets). In the tropics banana leaves are widely available, cut into squares and used as cheap throw-away plates or picked off the tree as ready-made umbrellas under which to shelter from tropical downpours. Here they make a glamorous wrapping for cod flavoured with lemon grass and kaffir lime leaves. Greaseproof paper can be substituted for the banana leaf, though this lacks the visual appeal.

Ingredients (serves four)

3 shallots
2 lemon grass stalks
1 large section of banana leaf
450 g/1 lb cod fillet
salt
1 tbsp peanut oil
8 kaffir lime leaves

Preheat oven to Gas Mark
5/375F/190C.

Banana Leaves

Peel and finely chop shallots. Peel tough outer leaves off lemon grass stalks. Finely chop white bulbous part, discarding the tough top part of the stalks. Blend or pound the shallots and lemon grass into a paste. Dip the banana leaf in boiling water briefly to soften it, drain and wipe dry.

Season cod fillet with salt. Brush with peanut oil. Spread out the banana leaf glossy side down on a flat baking sheet. Brush the banana leaf surface lightly with oil. Place the cod fillet in the centre of the oiled leaf, skin side-down. Spread the lemon grass paste over the cod and top with the kaffir lime leaves. Fold the banana leaf over the cod fillet to form a parcel, sealing the folds with cocktail sticks.

Bake for 30 minutes and serve straight from the oven. As you unwrap the banana leaf a wonderful citrus fragrance wafts up.

WINGED BEANS IN OYSTER SAUCE

One of the distinctive vegetables found in Thai supermarkets is winged beans, bright green beans with four frilly ridges running down their lengths. Here they are quickly cooked in an extremely simple stir-fry which keeps their crisp crunchiness intact.

Ingredients (serves four as a side-dish)

350 g/¾ lb winged beans
2 cloves garlic
1 tbsp groundnut oil
2 tbsp oyster sauce
1 tbsp soy sauce

Top and tail the winged beans and slice into short sections. Peel and roughly chop the garlic.

Heat a wok. Add in oil. Fry garlic until fragrant. Add in winged beans and stir-fry for 2-3 minutes. Add in oyster sauce and soy sauce. Stir-fry briefly, mixing well, then serve at once.

COCONUT ICE-CREAM SUNDAE

A speedy but scrumptious dessert. Packets of shredded young coconut are among the goodies to be found in the freezers at Thai supermarkets. These fine white shreds of coconut have a delicious fresh flavour and combine well with the rich sweetness of tinned jackfruit, lychees and bright pink rose syrup, also found in Thai shops.

Ingredients (serves four)

450 g/1 lb packet of frozen shredded young coconut, thawed
565 g tin of jackfruit in syrup
425 g tin of lychees in syrup
500 ml tub of good quality vanilla ice-cream
2 tbsp evaporated milk
2 tbsp rose syrup (optional)

Drain the shredded young coconut, jackfruit and lychees.

Scoop the ice-cream into four serving dishes. Top with young coconut shreds, jackfruit and lychees. Pour over evaporated milk and rose syrup. Serve at once.

BLACK RICE PUDDING WITH MANGO

Glutinous black rice (sold in Thai and Chinese supermarkets) is used to make a number of desserts in South East Asian cooking and is very much a comfort food. Here it is combined with rich coconut milk and juicy mango, making a pleasant end to a meal.

Ingredients (serves four)

200 g/7 oz glutinous black rice
1.2 ltr/2 pt water
2 tbsp soft dark brown sugar
2 mangoes
400 ml tin of coconut milk
pinch of salt

Rinse the rice. Place in a large saucepan together with the water and sugar. Bring to the boil. Cover and simmer for 30 minutes, stirring now and then. Uncover and simmer for a further 20-30 minutes stirring often until the rice has a porridge-like consistency.

Prepare the mangoes by cutting off the two fleshy 'cheeks' on either side of the large central stone (suck the flesh from the stones – cook's perks!). Slice the mango flesh into small cubes and scoop out of the skin. Mix the coconut milk well and stir in a pinch of salt.

Divide the warm glutinous rice among four serving dishes. Pour over coconut milk and top with mango cubes. Serve at once.

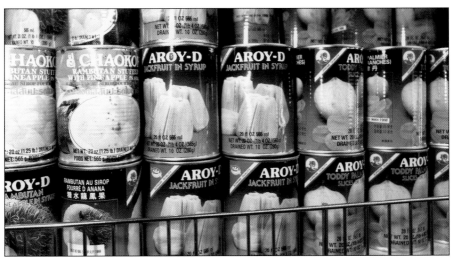

Tinned Jackfruit

127

RECOMMENDED COOKBOOKS

Charmaine Solomon's Thai Cookbook,
A clearly written collection of Thai recipes with appetising photographs of some of the dishes.

Thai Cooking,
Jennifer Brennan.
A classic book on Thai cooking, lovingly and knowledgeably written.

THAI GLOSSARY

Banana leaves: used to wrap foods in a similiar way to kitchen foil, but also adding flavour to whatever is cooked within.

Bean curd (tahu, tokua): a nutritious soya-bean product. Fresh ivory-coloured bean curd has a firm custard texture and bland flavour and is sold packed in water. Deep-fried bean curd has a golden colour and spongy texture. Both are found in the chilled section.

Candlenuts (kemiri, buah keras): large, white, waxy nuts, used to thicken curry pastes, sold unshelled. Raw macadamia nuts are the closest substitute.

Chilli paste (nam prik pow): a thick sauce made from chillies, onions and sugar.

Chillies (prik, cabe, sili labuyo): Introduced from South America via the Portuguese and Spanish in the 16th-century, chillies are an essential ingredient in South-East Asian cookery. Generally the smallest are the hottest, for instance, the tiny Thai bird's eye chillies.

Coconut milk (santen): this thick white 'milk' is made from the grated flesh of the coconut and not from the cloudy water found inside the coconut. In South-East Asia freshly-made coconut milk is sold in markets; here tinned coconut milk is the best option widely available. Creamed coconut and coconut milk powder, both of which need mixing with hot water, are the other options.

Coriander (cilantro, Chinese parsley, daun ketumbar, pak chee): this green flat-leafed herb, similar in appearance to continental parsley, has a distinctive sharp flavour. Both the seeds and the leaves are used throughout South-East Asia.

Fish sauce (nam pla, nuoc mam, patis): a thin, brown salty liquid, produced from compressed shrimps or small fish, and used similarly to soy sauce as a salty flavouring.

Galingale (Siamese ginger, lenguas, languas, ka): a fleshy rhizome, resembling a creamy-coloured root ginger with pink nodules, and a sharp, medicinal aroma. Available fresh or dried, either in pieces or in powder form (Laos powder).

Jackfruit: bulky, football-sized fruit with a thick green skin covered in prickles, similar in appearance to durian. Yellow jackfruit flesh is available tinned.

Kaffir limes (jeruk purut, makrut): large limes with a bumpy, dark-green skin. The glossy lime leaves are used in South-East Asian cooking and add a distinctive citrus flavour.

Krachai (lesser galingal): brown-skinned aromatic tubers which grow in clusters of 'fingers'.

Lemon grass (serai, sereh, takrai): a fibrous grey-green grass with a white bulbous base and subtle citrus flavour.

Mango: an orange-fleshed, fragrant fruit, eaten fresh and used in desserts. Pale orange Thai mangoes are particularly prized for their delicate flavour and scoopable flesh.

Mangosteen: an apple-sized fruit with thick purple skin which, despite its name, is no relation to the mango. Inside it contains white pulpy segments with a delicate flavour.

Noodles: cellophane noodles (also known as beanthread, glass or transparent noodles) are fine threadlike noodles made from mung beans and need soaking before they can be easily cut; yellow egg noodles (available fresh and dried); dried white rice noodles and vermicelli; river rice or sarhor noodles, made from ground rice and water. Fresh river rice noodles are sold in clear packets, usually stored near the chilled section.

Pandan leaves: long, thin, dark-green screwpine leaves, sold fresh in bunches. They add a unique, slightly nutty flavour and green colouring to desserts.

Rice: long-grain rice is commonly used, with the best coming from Thailand. The phrase 'perfumed rice' is an indicator of quality. Short-grained white and black glutinous rice is also used in both savoury and sweet dishes.

Shrimps, dried: small, shelled, dried pink shrimps, with a strong salty flavour.

Shrimp paste (blachan, terasi, bagoong, kapee, mam tan): a paste made from fermented shrimps, available in many forms, from solid, brown blocks to bottled pink-grey liquid. It has an extremely pungent smell and should be stored in an airtight container.

Soy sauce: a dark brown, salty liquid made from fermented soya beans, available as thin, salty Light Soy Sauce or as thicker, sweeter Dark Soy Sauce. Kecap manis is a thick, sweet Indonesian soy sauce.

Starfruit (carambola): a ridged, fruit which when sliced across forms star-shaped slices.

Tamarind (asam, mak kum): a bean-like fruit from the tamarind tree, available in lumps of de-seeded pulp, and used to add tartness to dishes. Tamarind sauce, although slightly salty, is a convenient version. 'Tamarind slices', from a different fruit with similar qualities, is also available.

Yard-long beans: as the name implies, these are indeed long green beans, commonly cut into short lengths before cooking.

EXOTIC FISH: THREE RECIPES

WINE-BAKED RED SNAPPERS
FRIED POMFRET WITH SWEET-SOUR CHILLI SAUCE
RAVIV'S TOMATO-BAKED GROUPER

London's fishmongers increasingly offer a range of tropical fishes, garnered from all around the world. While some are expensive, reflecting air-freight costs and luxury status, there are bargains to be found for the adventurous fish-eater.

There are several fishmongers at Brixton Market all selling a rainbow-bright assortment of fish including snapper, parrot fish and bream. Alternately, Golborne Fisheries, 75 Golborne Road, W11 (0181-960 3100) and France Fresh Fish, 99 Stroud Green Road, N14 (0171-263 9767) also have an excellent range of tropical fish.

Red Snapper

WINE-BAKED RED SNAPPERS

Red snappers, widely available in Brixton Market, are also increasingly found in fishmongers throughout London, where they make a colourful addition to the fish slab. Here they are baked with an assortment of vegetables, herbs and dry white wine.

Serve with rice and a vegetable side-dish. For a Caribbean flavour to the meal start with the Callaloo Soup (p.4) or Crab-stuffed Christophene (p.5).

Ingredients (serves four)

2 red onions
1 clove garlic
8 tomatoes
1 green pepper (the thin-skinned variety if possible)
a small bunch of fresh coriander
2 red snappers (each about 350 g/12 oz in weight) cleaned and gutted
salt and freshly ground pepper
6 sprigs of fresh thyme
juice of 1 lime
4 tbsp olive oil
300 ml/½ pt dry white wine

Preheat oven to Gas Mark 7/425F/220C.

Peel onions and slice into fine rings. Peel and chop garlic. Slice tomatoes across into fine slices. De-seed green pepper and slice into strips. Chop coriander.

Rinse snappers. Pat dry. Season with salt and freshly ground pepper.

Lightly oil an ovenproof serving dish. Place a layer of onion rings in the dish. Lay the snapper on top of the onion. Top the snapper with onion, garlic, tomato, green pepper, coriander and sprigs of thyme.

Pour over lime juice, olive oil and white wine. Bake for 40-50 minutes until the fish is cooked through.

FRIED POMFRET WITH SWEET-SOUR CHILLI SAUCE

Pomfret are tropical sea fish, silvery-white in colour, with firm white flesh, eaten widely in Asia. Fresh pomfret are sold at Good Harvest Fish & Meat fishmongers in Chinatown while competitively-priced packets of frozen pomfret can be found in Chinese supermarkets (though these usually need cleaning and gutting).

This tasty dish with its flavourful chilli sauce goes well with boiled white rice and a side-vegetable such as Black Bean Water Spinach (p.43) or stir-fried beansprouts.

Ingredients (serves four)

2 red chillies	*4 tbsp flour*
2 cloves garlic	*oil for shallow-frying*
2.5 cm/1 in root ginger	*2 tbsp light soy sauce*
2 tsp cornflour	*2 tbsp rice vinegar*
2 tbsp water	*2 tbsp sugar*
4 spring onions	*2 tbsp tomato puree*
¼ red pepper	*a few sprigs of fresh coriander*
4 pomfret (each around 250 g/9 oz)	
cleaned and gutted	
salt and freshly ground pepper	

Chop chillies, discarding stems. Peel and chop garlic and ginger. Blend or grind chilli, garlic and ginger into paste.

Mix cornflour with water. Trim spring onions and chop into fine 2.5 cm/1 inch long shreds. Chop red pepper into short fine strips

Rinse pomfret and pat dry. Cut slashes in the thickest part of the pomfret. Season with salt and pepper. Lightly coat with flour.

Heat oil in a large frying pan. Fry pomfret until golden-brown on each side and cooked through. Remove with a slotted spoon to a serving dish.

While the pomfret is frying make the sauce. Heat 1 tbsp oil in a small saucepan. Fry chilli paste in the oil until fragrant. Add in soy sauce, rice vinegar, sugar, tomato puree and 1 tsp salt. Mix and cook gently for 3 minutes. Bring to the boil. Remove from heat. Mix in cornflour paste, stirring until well mixed.

Sprinkle spring onion shreds, red pepper strips and coriander sprigs over the fried pomfret. Pour over the chilli sauce and serve at once.

RAVIV'S TOMATO-BAKED GROUPER

This is Raviv Goldman's version of a Moroccan dish called chraima which he first ate in Israel. The original dish was so chilli-hot and spicy that it practically brought tears to his eyes, this version, while still flavourful, is mild in comparison.

The grouper is found in warm seas, from the Mediterranean to the Indian Ocean and there are several varieties, sometimes sold according to colour such as red or yellow grouper. Brixton Market or Golborne Fisheries at 75 Golborne Road, W10 (0181-960 3100) are likely sources.

Given the intensely flavourful tomato sauce in which the grouper is cooked, Raviv recommends serving it simply with rice and a side-salad.

Ingredients (serves four)

1 head of garlic
1 red pepper
1 tomato
1 small bunch of flat-leaf parsley
1 small bunch of coriander
50 ml/2 fl oz oil
50 ml/2 fl oz lemon juice
100 g/3½ oz tomato puree
1 tbsp paprika
½ tsp ground chilli
1 tsp salt
1 tsp ground cumin
1 cardamom pod
700 g/1½ lb filleted grouper

Peel and chop the garlic cloves. De-seed the red pepper and chop into strips. Chop the tomato, parsley and coriander.

Heat the oil in a large heavy-bottomed casserole dish. Fry the garlic until golden-brown. Add in the red pepper and fry for 1-2 minutes. Add in the tomato, lemon juice, tomato puree, parsley, coriander, paprika, chilli, salt, cumin and cardamom, mixing well. Bring to the boil and cook over medium heat until thickened. Add in the grouper fillets, adding water if needed to cover the fish with liquid. Cover and simmer gently for 10-15 minutes until the fish is cooked through. Check the seasoning and adjust accordingly. Serve either hot or cold.

KITCHEN SHOPS

CENTRAL LONDON

The Chef Shop, Bluebird Foodmarket
350 King's Road, SW3
(0171-559 1112)
Open: Mon-Sat 9am-9pm, Sun 11am-5pm
Part of Conran's new gastrodrome in the
beautifully-restored vintage garage is a
light and airy kitchenware shop, billed as
the sort of shop chefs might shop in for
their kitchens at home. Stock includes an
array of top-notch cookware and cookery
books.

Divertimenti
45-7 Wigmore Street, W1
(0171-935 0689)
Open: Mon-Fri 9.30am-6pm, Sat 10am-6pm
An attractive shop with a seductive
combination of colourful ceramic
tableware and cooking utensils. The
Fulham Road branch also holds cooking
demonstrations by some of the leading
lights in the food world.
Also at: 139-141 Fulham Road, SW3 (0171-
581 8065). Open: Mon-Fri 9.30am-6pm, Sat
10am-6pm

Elizabeth David Cookshop
3 North Row
Covent Garden, WC2
(0171-836 9167)
Tube: Covent Garden
Open: Mon-Fri 10.30am-6.30pm, Sat 10am-
7pm, Sun 12noon-5pm
Offers an extensive range of Le Creuset
cookware, plus gadgets, cookbooks and
tableware.

Jerry's Home Store
163-167 Fulham Road, SW3
(0171-581 0909)
Tube: South Kensington
Open: Mon-Sat 10am-6pm, Sun 12noon-6pm
A bright and airy all-American store with a
fine line in cheerful tableware, American
cookbooks and kitchen utensils and
gadgets including Waring blenders, pizza
baking tins and popcorn makers.

Leon Jaeggi
77 Shaftesbury Avenue, W1
(0171-580 1974/434 4545)
Tube: Leicester Square/Piccadilly Circus
Open: Mon-Sat 9am-5.30pm
A distinctly professional affair, aimed at
the catering trade and frequented by chefs.
Stock is extensive and the staff are helpful
and knowledgeable. Note that prices do
not include VAT.

Newport Supermarket
28-29 Newport Court, WC2
(0171-437 2386)
Tucked away down this Chinatown side-
alley this shop specialises in Chinese
cookware and tableware, from woks and
bamboo steamers to rice cookers.

Pages
121 Shaftesbury Avenue, W1
(0171-379 6334)
Open: Mon-Fri 9am-6pm, Sat 9am-5pm
A large well-stocked shop aimed at the
professional catering trade.

NORTH LONDON

Gill Wing Cookshop
190 Upper Street, N1
(0171-226 5392)
Friendly and well-established with stock
ranging from stainless steel saucepans to
decorative tableware.

Richard Dare
93 Regent's Park Road, NW1
(0171-722 9428)
Open: Mon-Fri 9.30am-6pm, Sat 10am-4pm
Primrose Hill residents are well-served by
this attractive shop: upstairs is practical
cookware, from knives to saucepans, while
downstairs is the basement crammed with
colourful French ceramic tableware.

The Scullery
123 Muswell Hill Broadway, N10
(0181-444 5236)
Open: Mon-Sat 9am-6pm, Sun 12noon-4pm
A small, cheerful kitchenware shop with
colourful stock such as straw baskets,
picnic hampers and huge candles spilling
out onto the pavement in front.

Yaohan Plaza
399 Edgware Road, NW9
(0181-200 0009)
Open: Mon-Fri 9am-7pm, Sat 10am-9pm, Sun
12noon-6pm
If you're in search of Japanese cookware
then look no further. Yaohan has
everything from ginger graters and sushi
mats to rectangular frying pans and shabu
shabu pots.

SOUTH LONDON

Cookshop
89 The Broadway, SW19
(0181-543 1010)
Open: Mon-Fri 9.30am-5.30pm, Sat 9.30am-6pm
An all-round cookshop selling stock from
baking tins to woks.

La Cuisiniere
81-83 Northcote Road, SW11
(0171-223 4487)
Open: Mon-Sat 9.30am-6pm
Run on the premises that "life goes on in
the kitchen" stock here ranges from
tableware to specialist gadgets.

Kooks Unlimited
16 Eton Street, Richmond
(0181-940 8448)
Open: Mon-Sat 9.30am-5.30pm
A small cheerful shop (as the name
suggests), crammed with an array of
cook's essentials.

WEST LONDON

John Russell Kitchenware
128 Chiswick High Road, W4
(0181-994 5790)
Open: Mon-Sat 10am-6pm
A small, well-stocked shop with
perceptively chosen stock.

Kitchen Ideas
70 Westbourne Grove, W2
(0171-229 3388)
Open Mon-Sat 9.30am-6pm
A large down-to-earth shop with shop
aimed primarily at the catering trade.
Also at 23 New Broadway W5 (0181-566
5620); Open Mon-Sat 930am-6pm

The Kitchenware Company
36 Hill Street
Richmond
(0181-948 7785)
Open: Mon-Sat 9.30am-5.30pm
A well-stocked shop with stock from
everyday basics to specialist equipment.

BOOKSHOPS

The Africa Centre
38 King Street, WC2
(0171-240 6649)
Open: Mon-Fri 11am-5.30pm, Sat 11am-5pm
A useful source of hard-to-find African
cookbooks.

Books for Cooks
4 Blenheim Crescent, W11
(0171-221 1992)
Open: Mon-Sat 9.30am-6pm
This tiny shop, crammed with cookbooks
from floor to ceiling, is a mecca for anyone
interested in food and cookery. The stock
is impressively international, covering
cuisines around the world and including
American publications and an out-of-print
section. At the back of the shop recipes are
tested in a small kitchen area, resulting in
mouth watering aromas wafting through
the shop. Dining space is limited to a few
tables and chairs – so get there early for
lunch. Staff are both knowledgeable and
helpful.

The Japan Centre
212 Piccadilly, W1
(0171-434 4218)
Open: Mon-Sat 10am-7.30pm, Sun 10am-6pm
A good selection of Japanese cookbooks,
many of them attractively illustrated.

Orbis Books
66 Kenway Road, SW5
(0171-370 2210)
Open: Mon-Fri 9.30am-5.30pm, Sat
9.30am-4.30pm
A Polish bookshop with some imported
Polish cookbooks.

Index

METRO PUBLICATIONS

PO Box 6336
London
N1 6PY
Tel/Fax: 0181 802 7573

Bargain Hunters' London
Author: Andrew Kershman
£5.99, 144pp, 40 b/w photos, 12 Maps.
ISBN 0-9522914-2-8

Bargain Hunters' London reviews over 500 bargain outlets. Within its pages you can find just about any item (new or used), as well as tips about bartering and maps to help plan bargain days out in the capital. Bargain Hunters' features designer sales, electrical wholesalers, cheap street fashion, auctions, charity shops and much more.

Gay London
Author: Graham Parker
£5.99, 144pp, 40 b/w photos, 4 Maps,
ISBN 0-9522914-6-0

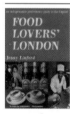

Gay London includes reviews of all the social clubs, political organisations, health services, restaurants and night clubs to help gay men enjoy the Capital. The book is an essential reference manual for those wishing to explore the capital's gay scene, and the most up to date book of its kind.

Food Lovers' London
Author: Jenny Linford
£5.99, 144pp, 40 b/w photos.
ISBN 0-9522914-5-2

Food Lovers' London contains all the information a London foodie needs to start cooking any of the thirteen nationalities of cuisine featured. Each cuisine has a glossary of ingredients and reviews of all the best food shops and eating places, as well as a brief history of the people and culture that gave rise to the food.

The London Market Guide
Author: Andrew Kershman
£3.99, 80pp, 60 b/w photos, 80 Maps.
ISBN 0-9522914-0-1

The London Market Guide contains all the essential information to explore London's 70 street markets with maps, photos, travel information, consumer tips, over 90 cafes and full contact details for those wanting to get a stall. The more popular markets like Portobello and Camden receive special attention, with details about the best days to visit if you want to avoid the crowds, and detailed maps.

Veggie London
Author: Craig John Wilson
£5.99, 112pp, 30 b/w photos.
ISBN 0-9522914-1-X

Craig Wilson has reviewed over 120 of the capital's vegetarian restaurants, in an attempt to escape from the veggie burger and find the best in vegetarian cuisine. Many of the restaurants listed also serve meat (for those who don't mind socialising with carnivores). The book also includes wholefood stores, vegetarian caterers, social and pressure groups.